Above the Apparent and Beyond the Present

A MASTERY OF LIFE

Anna Zibarras

"It is the mark of an educated mind to be able to entertain a thought without accepting it."

—Aristotle

WestBow
PRESS
A DIVISION OF THOMAS NELSON

This book is a nonprofit project. Proceeds will be given to humanitarian and charitable causes for the Glory of God and for the benefit of all.

WestBow Press books may be ordered through booksellers or by contacting:

WestBow Press
A Division of Thomas Nelson
1663 Liberty Drive
Bloomington, IN 47403
www.westbowpress.com
1-(866) 928-1240

ISBN: 978-1-4497-0789-7 (sc)
ISBN: 978-1-4497-0699-9 (dj)
ISBN: 978-1-4497-0698-2 (e)

Library of Congress Control Number: 2010940239

Printed in the United States of America

WestBow Press rev. date: 01/13/2011

Dedicated to my beloved husband, my most precious children, and my wonderful grandchildren, Alexander and Jason for the purpose of advancing their consciousness, for their spiritual fulfillment, and for enlightenment in their lives.

May the lives they will lead be a reflection of the morals and ideals mentioned in this book.

Contents

Acknowledgment

I would like to express my love and gratitude to my husband, without whom this book would not have been written and finalized, to my children, for their continuous support and encouragement, and to all my dear friends for their faith in me, my principles, and my ideas.

Introduction

"We are evolving from five-sensory humans into multisensory humans. Our five senses together form a single sensory system that is designed to perceive physical reality. The perceptions of a multisensory human extend beyond physical reality to the larger dynamical systems of which our physical reality is a part."

—GARY ZUKAV

Spiritual Development

"O God, you are my God, I seek you, my
soul thirsts for you;" (Psalm 63:1)

Some people have a natural, innate urge to search for spiritual development. Although it is a long process that needs effort, goodwill, and persistence, it eventually leads the devotees to their inner treasure house of beauty, love and peace.

My Search

For the last thirty six years, after my realization that we are more than physical beings, I have been searching for spiritual teachings and I have been researching the spiritual resources of "Esoteric Christianity," through both formal and informal networks of teachers and scholars who were happy to share their findings and knowledge with me.

During all this time, I very often felt an urge to discover a spiritual path that I could apply in a practical way to my everyday life, one that would lead me to the divine—to the kingdom of heaven—which starts here and now, and carries on into eternity.

I very soon realised that spiritual development is what enables one to tap on the enormous powers that exist in the universe. It is what fulfils one's wishes, what renders joy, happiness, bliss, and the kingdom of God on Earth. Without spiritual development, one has no mastery over one's life; one has no guidance and no direction. A person is the victim of his own thoughts and delusions. He is like a boat in the middle of an ocean that is left without oars or without engine or sails.

My Findings

As I progressed and as I came across concepts such as elevated consciousness, elevated awareness, spiritual unity, inner peace, and divine harmony, I became more and more excited, more interested, and more curious to discover and experience in depth each and every one of these concepts.

What I found fascinating was that most, if not all, of the spiritual paths teach their followers high moral discipline as the first step in the path to opening one's consciousness to the divine and to attaining "Nirvana."

Moral discipline is simply the conscious awareness and determination to avoid acts that cause harm to oneself and to others, and to concentrate on practicing virtuous acts for the benefit of all.

"Peace, My Peace, I give you," said Jesus. (John 14:27) Without peace of mind, happiness remains elusive. According to Christian teachings, our happiness depends on the degree of faith we carry, the love we share, and the compassion we feel. By acting with love for our fellow human beings, by showing attitudes of patience and compassion toward others, we attract the grace of God, which enlightens us and takes care of us.

"Devote yourselves to prayer, keeping alert in it with an attitude of thanksgiving," Paul wrote to the Colossians (4:2). Meditation and prayer are shortcuts that lead us to our inner state of beauty, and peace. They are the keys to our enlightenment and the godly attitudes of love, patience, and compassion. Through meditation and prayer, we can experience improved human relationships, enhanced creativity, better communication, greater opportunities, and easier access to the kingdom of heaven on Earth.

Chapter 1

Attitude

Attitudes are more important than facts!

— KARL MENNINGER

Attitude is an ongoing dynamic state of mind.

After studying human psychology and observing human behavior for many years, I came to the conclusion that our own attitude can affect our reality, personality, health, and relationships with others.

> I am determined to be cheerful and happy in whatever situation I may find myself. For I have learned that the greater part of our misery or unhappiness is determined not by our circumstance but by our disposition (Martha Washington).

Attitude Alters Reality

I have also noticed that our attitude has the ability to distort our reality, which means that in our everyday lives, we have the ability, through our own minds, to see only what we wish to see.

Some individuals perceive only beauty, goodness, and opportunities. Others only see threats, persecution, wickedness, and failure around them, to which they react accordingly.

Your Good Attitude Makes You Attractive

It is amazing that a good attitude is more important than looks or talent, as it can even transcend one's shortcomings, physical characteristics and mental problems! Normally people tend to be more attracted to those who possess a positive attitude in spite of their other possible problems in life.

In contrast, a negative attitude which is a complete lack of enthusiasm and consequently, a lack of creativity and inspiration in a person becomes a natural repellent.

Unfortunately, when we have a very busy schedule and an unbalanced life, our attitude and hence, our pleasant personality can be affected. As a result, even our most attractive physical characteristics can be minimized by our negative attitude and a bad mood.

Attitude Is Never Static

It is noticeable in our behavior, and in the behavior of others around us, that our attitude keeps shifting all the time, from degrees of negativity to degrees of positivity.

Unfortunately, no one can maintain a good attitude all the time, as our positive attitudes are constantly threatened by personal disappointments, family problems, human conflict, health concerns, and negative self-images.

When this happens, our ability to produce, maintain, and restore a good attitude through conscious effort can make a very big difference in our everyday lives.

Success Depends on a Good Attitude

A positive and a loving attitude is the most powerful and priceless personality characteristic we can possess, as it can alter our life circumstances to a great extent.

Generally speaking, people who talk and act well and in a pleasant manner are more successful in life than those who display an unpleasant disposition. Pleasant, loving people also manage to get out of difficult situations in a much easier way.

People with a bad attitude and bad behavior poison every situation, even ones that are not necessarily bad.

After all, "You have achieved success if you have lived well, laughed often, and loved much" (author unknown).

What Is a Charismatic Personality?

A charismatic personality is what we call the combination of individual characteristics and behavioral traits that send out a certain magic or charm to others.

The effects of a charismatic personality in our everyday personal or business interactions are tremendous.

What Is Enthusiasm?

The word *enthusiasm*, which is derived from the Greek, *en Theos*, means the state or condition of being "in God." When you are enthused, you are within the positive energy of God, which flows through you.

> "Enthusiasm spells the difference between mediocrity
> and accomplishment," Norman Vincent Peale

Therefore, enthusiasm is an attractive power that connects us successfully with the living power of this universe and with other human beings.

You Can Control Your Attitude

Our attitude, good or bad, gets noticed immediately by the people around us in the different approaches we take and in the disposition that we communicate to them.

I found it fascinating to see how some people, with hardly any effort, can develop positive thoughts and a good attitude, no matter how difficult and complicated a situation is.

The benefits of being able to do so are tremendous, as when we are positive, we become enthusiastic, we can think better, and we can try harder.

When our expectations are high, when we expect good, good arises in most situations. When we expect success, we have many more possibilities to succeed. Therefore, it is our right attitude that creates our success and our happiness in life.

The Builder by author unknown, source unknown

An elderly builder had reached the age and stage of retirement.

His boss was very sorry to see one of his best workers go and asked him, as a last favor, to build just one more house.

The builder did not want to refuse, so he accepted. But, as he was doing it against his will, he ended up doing a quick and shoddy job, using inferior materials and cutting as many corners as possible. It was his last job, so nothing could jeopardize his career or influence his future employment opportunities.

When the house was finished, the builder called his employer to inspect it. To his amazement, his boss of twenty-five years handed him the keys to the front door. "This house is for you," he said, "as a sign of appreciation for everything you did for the company."

This is normally what happens when we do things in our lives with the wrong attitude, by reacting to others instead of acting independently and out of goodwill.

When we do not put our best effort into what we do, the situation we create may shock us and affect our future life.

Applications

1- Look at your life as a "do-it-yourself" project. Your present life could very well be the result of your attitudes and choices in the past. Consequently, your future will be the result of your attitudes and the choices you make today.

2- When your positive attitude is threatened due to conflict, whether in a family or work situation, try to solve it quickly with an apology or a discussion, or try to accept and forget it. Even better … laugh it off.

3- Avoid people who bring and keep you down with their negative attitudes, in order to avoid further disappointment.

4- Give up the need to be right, in order to feel more at peace.

5- Alternatively, learn to ignore a negative or threatening situation for as long as possible. If someone says something negative or hurtful that affects and worries you, stop thinking about it. In reality, it can only affect you as long as you keep thinking about it. Remember that a negative comment can never hurt you without your permission!

6- You cannot control everything that happens in your life, but you can fully control how you react to it. You have the power to choose your response and achieve more peace and less stress in your life. Remember what Jimmy Dean said " I can't change the direction of the wind but I can adjust my sails to always reach my destination",

7- Do not react quickly when someone offends or hurts you. With time, the negative effects of every situation are minimized.

8- Have patience and faith. Pray for your enemies to be forgiven and released from negativity, greed, and a selfish attitude. The grace of God is attracted by the simple-hearted, patient people who humbly trust their heavenly Father and have confidence in Him rather than trusting their own thoughts, power, and control.

9- Trust in divine justice when treated unfairly, whatever the circumstances may be.

10- In times of trouble, try consciously to restore and maintain a good attitude through a few short moments of meditation on God's Love, which "is not irritable or resentful". (Paul 1 Cor. 13:5).

The justice of God cannot but reign. It may be delayed for a while, but sooner or later, it will appear in our lives. As long as we love our fellow human beings and we show attitudes of patience and compassion, we will attract the grace of God, which will take care of us.

Chapter 2

Love

Love a man even in his sin for that is the semblance of divine love and it is the highest love on Earth. Love all God's creations, the whole and every grain of sand in it. Love every leaf and every way of God's light. Love the animals, love the plants, love everything. If you love everything, you will perceive the Divine mystery in things. Once you perceive it, you will begin to comprehend it better every day and you will come at last to love the whole world with an all embracing love.

- DOSTOYEVSKY, THE BROTHERS KARAMAZOV

"Whoever does not love does not know God, for God is love."

(1 JOHN: 8)

Love Is Energy

Since my early years, I have felt that love is the most powerful energy in the world, and to experience this energy in any form would be the most intriguing and the most wonderful thing that could happen in my life.

Soon, I realized intuitively that the power of love exists within all of us. It acts like a stream of electricity, as an inner, motivating force, which enables us to offer many wonderful things to ourselves and to those around us. It enables us to give to the people we love:

1. the happiness of our recognition, which gives them the strength they need to carry on in life,

2. the pleasure of our appreciation, which acts as a great stimulus for growth and development,
3. the joy of our acceptance, which allows them the freedom to dream, as well as the power to achieve their dreams,
4. the peace of our attention, which enables them to accept situations, to forget hurts, to heal wounds, to settle disputes, and to carry on with their lives.

When we give love, we attract love. When we create harmony, we attract harmony. When we forgive, we get forgiven. Spreading love and forgiveness sets us free from unwanted negative thoughts and feelings and enables us to fulfill the call of God and our purpose in this life.

Types and degrees of love

Although love is an infinite connection between two or more loving souls, and although we all have the same need to give and to receive love, the quality of love is subjective and can differ not only from person to person but also at different times within the same person as to its frequency, intensity, duration, and spiritual quality.

Unfortunately, love cannot be demanded or commanded or purchased or controlled. It is earned only by a good, unselfish, positive, loving, and giving attitude that expects nothing in return. We have to give love in order to receive love, and the only way to get the whole world to love us is to love the whole world ourselves first.

Falling in Love

Being in love is a state of the mind obsessed with mystery, infatuation, and desire. When two people fall in love, their perception gets distorted to such an extent that they create a perfect myth about each other based on an exaggerated image of good qualities and attributes beyond any relevance to reality and any recognition.

The more obsessive one's desire becomes, the more distorted the perception gets and the more exaggerated the qualities of the other person become. In reality, people fall in love not exactly with the other person but with the image that they themselves have created in their minds and have projected onto the other person.

This universal phenomenon of falling in love with a person or the strong desire to possess somebody in order to find happiness and fulfillment lies in the fact that people tend to look outside themselves for somebody or something that will make them feel complete and whole.

In such a situation, as soon as the infatuation and the desire are fulfilled, and one's perception becomes less and less distorted, one starts to realize that what one hoped for and what one got are two different things. The result is sometimes an awful disappointment. What follows next is a new need to start looking for a substitute, for someone or something on which new expectations are placed in search of fulfillment and happiness again.

It is important to understand that long-lasting and fully satisfying relationships require two fully self-actualized, whole, and fulfilled people, relying on real inner love and commitment and not on the need for each other in order to make them complete. "The best relationship is one in which your love for each other exceeds your need for each other," the Dalai Lama said.

What Happens When We Are Denied Love

When people are denied their fundamental need to give and receive love, they become angry, and they end up experiencing much unhappiness, selfishness, inadequacy, inferiority, and loneliness in their lives. This naturally interferes with their progress to attain their full potential and spiritual evolution.

Anger Is Destructive

Anger destroys the quality of our life, blocks out our logic, and leads us to say and do things that unfortunately will be impossible to undo.

Anger is based on our mind's perception of what someone said or did. Thinking about it normally tends to prolong and reinforce our anger rather than pacify us, and it creates vengeful thoughts and actions which are much more likely to create hostilities and interfere with logic rather than solve a problem.

"Holding on to anger is like grasping a hot coal with the intent of throwing it at someone else; you are the one who gets burned," Buddha said. Holding a grudge can only fill our hearts with bitterness and revenge, causing great harm, disharmony, and illness in us.

Who Makes Us Angry?

No one *makes* us angry. Anger is our internal emotional response to some outside action or event. Anyone can be a target for an angry person. "You must understand this, my beloved: let everyone be quick to listen, slow to speak, slow to anger; for your anger does not produce God's righteousness". (James 1:19-20)

The Nails in the Fence <u>Author Unknown, found online at Inspiration Peak.com</u>

There once was a young man who could not control his anger. His teacher gave him some nails and told him that every time he could not control his anger, instead of losing his temper and misbehaving, he should instead run to the wooden fence and hammer a nail into it. The young man obeyed his teacher and did as he was told. The first day he put eight nails into the fence. During the next few days, as he became more aware of his anger and as he developed more control over his temper, gradually the number of nails hammered into the fence became fewer and fewer. He discovered it was easier to hold his temper than to drive those nails into the fence. Eventually, the day came when the boy didn't lose his temper at all. His teacher then suggested that he pull out one nail out for each time that he managed to control himself. When that task was completed too, the teacher went with the young man to the fence on which all the holes of the removed nails remained and remarked, "You see, my boy, although you have removed all the nails that you had hammered in, the fence will never be the same again. The holes that you have created will always remain like scars, behind. When you say things in anger, they leave a scar just like this one and unfortunately no word of apology can ever restore these wounds."

"A fool gives full vent to anger, but the wise
quietly holds it back" (Proverbs 29:11).

What Should We Do?

The only answer and solution to anger is forgiveness. "To forgive is the highest, most beautiful form of love. In return, you will receive untold peace and happiness," Dr. Robert Muller said.

When you feel angry:

1. Try to find the highest feeling of love within yourself and let your consciousness guide your actions.
2. Realize that whenever you act with anger toward another person, you are acting against yourself first.
3. Release anger as soon as possible, in order to align yourself again with the positive flow of the energy of the universe and with its healing power.
4. Only by acting with empathy, tolerance, understanding, forgiving and forgetting, your mind will be liberated from the suffering that anger creates.

The Golden Rule

"Do to others as you would have them do to you. If you love those who love you, what credit is that to you? For even sinners love those who love them. If you do good to those who do good to you, what credit is that to you? For even sinners do the same. If you lend to those from whom you hope to receive, what credit is that to you? Even sinners lend to sinners, to receive as much again. But love your enemies, do good, and lend, expecting nothing in return. Your reward will be great, and you will be children of the Most High; for he is kind to the ungrateful and the wicked. Be merciful, just as your Father is merciful." (Luke 6:31-36)

What did Paul say?

"If I speak in the tongues of mortals and of angels, but do not have love, I am a noisy gong or a clanging cymbal. And if I have prophetic powers, and understand all mysteries and all knowledge, and if I have all faith, so as to remove mountains, but do not have love, I am nothing. If

I give away all my possessions, and if I hand over my body so that I may boast, but do not have love, I gain nothing. Love is patient; love is kind; love is not envious or boastful or arrogant or rude. It does not insist on its own way; it is not irritable or resentful; it does not rejoice in wrongdoing, but rejoices in the truth. It bears all things, believes all things, hopes all things, endures all things. Love never ends. (1 Corinthians 13:1–8)

What did Matthew say?

'You have heard that it was said, "You shall love your neighbor and hate your enemy." But I say to you, Love your enemies and pray for those who persecute you, so that you may be children of your Father in heaven; for he makes his sun rise on the evil and on the good, and sends rain on the righteous and on the unrighteous. For if you love those who love you, what reward do you have? Do not even the tax-collectors do the same? And if you greet only your brothers and sisters, what more are you doing than others? Do not even the Gentiles do the same? Be perfect, therefore, as your heavenly Father is perfect." (Matthew 5: 43-48)

Application

1- People are sensitive to love, to giving, to goodness, and to gratitude. If you want to live in a world of love, see the whole world with love instead of judgment.

2- Give love in order to attract love. Create harmony to attract harmony. Forgive in order to be forgiven.

3- Apply these attitudes in your daily lives and practice what you are reciting in the Lord's prayer that "His will shall be done on Earth as it is in heaven," for your lives to improve tremendously, and in order to feel loved, happy, and fulfilled.

4- Spread unlimited and unconditional love and forgiveness, in order to be set free from unwanted negative thoughts and feelings.

5- You will consequently realize that "Love bears all things, believes all things, hopes all things, endures all things," that "Love never ends," and that you are fulfilling the call of God and your purpose in this life.

Chapter 3

Faith

"So I tell you, whatever you ask for in prayer, believe
that you have received it, and it will be yours"

(MARK II: 24)

I have always been fascinated with the tremendous possibilities
and the new experiences we can be faced with when we take the time
and put the effort to develop our faith and work on it.

I have personally felt so many times the presence of God in my
daily life, and I have witnessed so many daily miracles—or you
could say prayers answered—that I am strongly convinced without
any doubt that there is another realm which transcends our physical
world and which can be attained through the power of our faith.

What Is Faith?

Faith is the belief that there is a non-physical dimension, an
invisible world, which is not perceived by the senses, which lies
beyond and above the seen world and is responsible for everything
that takes place in it.

Thomas Merton says, "Faith is the opening of an inward eye, the
eye of the heart, to be filled with the presence of the divine light."

"Faith is the single most important tool of man's existence." Dr.
Joyce Brothers said. It is a force or a divine spark within some of us
that draws us towards the truth.

What Does Faith Do?

Faith works as a thought force which, when focused in a particular direction, allows us to accept with certainty the fact that a higher intelligence is working through us and through everyone else for the good of all; that there is a purpose and a reason for everything, and that everything happens for the good of all.

Faith which enables us to realize our true potential, to turn the invisible to visible and the imagined to the actual, requires a continual inner effort, a continual altering of the mind, of the habitual ways of thought and of habitual reactions.

Faith is necessary in order to develop the part of our brain that is not stimulated by our senses and in order to modify the circumstances in which we live, assuming control over them rather than continuing to be directed by them and being controlled by them.

Within us we have talents and abilities that we are not aware of. Within us lies the cause of whatever enters into our lives. Our health and happiness depend on the degree of faith we carry, the love we share, and the compassion we feel.

Faith heals

A true event told by Marshall Dudley, following were all witnessed by Marshall Dudley. The people and healer wish to remain anonymous posted at the execonn.com:

"Gary was on the back of a motorcycle when a woman hit them head on, several years earlier. He spent months in the hospital, and although most of his injuries had healed, he had a ruptured disk that caused him unending pain. Often it would be so bad that he would have to leave work early.

"A co-worker offered to see if he could help with hands-on Christian healing, and although Gary was not certain if he believed it possible, he knew the doctors had told him there was nothing else they could do, so he decided to give it a try.

"Every time his pain became too much, he went to the co-worker, who put his hands on his back and prayed for his healing. The heat Gary felt in his body as a result of the laying of the praying hands on him was quite intense, and after a minute or two, the pain would subside. However, a few hours later, it would return. He was discouraged, because although the healing would work for a while, the pain would eventually return. However, over the next few weeks, the pain took longer and longer to return, and was less and less severe. After five or six weeks, the pain was gone for good.

"Gary returned to the doctor for his periodic checkup. The doctor was astounded that the ruptured disk had healed! According to him, ruptured disks do not heal. When pressed for an explanation, the doctor said that the only possible explanation could be that obviously there had been a mix-up on his X-rays before (every time they took them) and that the file X-rays were of someone else. However, Gary and I know the truth."

Faith Makes You Powerful

"So I tell you, whatever you ask for in prayer, believe that you have received it, and it will be yours." (Mark 11;24)

By having faith, which is accomplished by continuous prayer to God, we can achieve and receive anything we wish, as faith and communication with God can activate the greatest power on earth and in the heavens, providing us with the key to every success, inner peace, and absolute joy in our lives.

A Miracle of Faith Healing in Vancouver

Catholic Church investigates inexplicable healing of dying man. Rev. John Horgan knew a dying man when he saw one. Years of working as a chaplain in Vancouver General and St. Paul's hospitals had seen to that.

So when he saw Peter Andersen in Vancouver General's intensive care unit on the afternoon of July 3, 2008, he didn't need anyone to tell him that Andersen's situation was grave. His bloodstream was teeming with the bacteria from two flesh-eating diseases: myositis, which attacks the muscles, and necrotizing fasciitis, which invades the flesh beneath the skin.

Andersen, on life support, was bloated beyond recognition from septic shock. Whole muscle groups of dead tissue had been stripped away by surgeons from his right leg. His blood pressure was so low it was in the range that indicates imminent death, and his kidneys and other organs had failed.

He appeared to be within hours of dying.

But what happened next is going to lead to a formal investigation by the Catholic Church to determine if the spiritual intervention of an Irish-French monk, Columba Marmion who died in 1923, was responsible for a medical miracle.

Because Andersen didn't die. He made a recovery that at first sight seems to defy medicine and logic.

The canonical investigation of Andersen's healing could lead to the canonization of the monk as a saint.

On June 30 last year, Andersen suddenly developed a high fever and complained of a pain in his leg. The next day, the pain became unbearable.

"I remember them putting me in the ambulance, but after that I lost consciousness for two weeks," Andersen said, describing it as an awful darkness.

Until he developed what appeared to be the flu, Peter was a healthy, strapping individual, Charlene said.

"The surgeons removed bagfuls of dead tissue and muscle and he'd had two skin grafts. Then he contracted severe septic shock syndrome, which caused his body to bloat like a balloon. I asked them, 'Can you save him?' and one surgeon said, 'We are trying, but no, he's not going to make it.' I pleaded with them to take his leg off but they said it was too late for that."

Charlene sent for Horgan, the couple's parish priest, who had introduced them to books written by Marmion, who was given the title "Blessed" based on a miraculous cure attributed to prayers for his intercession.

Horgan arrived carrying with him a relic of Marmion—a fragment of his monk's habit.

The priest was gowned and masked and led into intensive care unit.

"I asked Blessed Marmion to intercede with the Lord and bring healing," said Horgan.

At mass the next day, he asked the congregation to pray for a miracle for Andersen, "as this was his only hope."

Charlene didn't believe her husband would survive: "I knew he was going to die and I didn't believe a miracle was going to happen, my faith wasn't strong enough. The charge nurse told me he was at the point of death."

But Peter didn't die that Thursday, or the Friday. On Saturday, five days after he fell ill, a nurse rushed up to Charlene.

"He was really excited. He said, 'The blood culture's come back and it's negative. I'm taking him off life support.' He pulled the tube out of his mouth and Peter said to me, 'Can you give me a hug?'"

One of his surgeons told Charlene her husband's recovery was a miracle, another said he was very lucky.

He would be in hospital for the next four months. Doctors told her he would never walk again or drive a car, and a psychiatrist told her he would likely be brain-damaged—none of which happened. He has returned to work as the pastoral care director of Columbus Residence, a care facility for the elderly in south Vancouver.

News of his inexplicable recovery eventually spread to Marmion's former abbey in Belgium and to an Irish priest, Rev. Mark Tierney of County Limerick, who is promoting Marmion's cause for sainthood.

Blessed Marmion was born in Dublin in 1858 and was a diocesan priest until he entered Maredsous Abbey in Belgium, where he became abbot in 1909. He wrote a number of books, including *Christ, the Life of the Soul,* that are considered spiritual classics. A Benedictine abbey in Illinois is named after him.

Both the Maredsous Abbey and Tierney have asked the archdiocese to launch a formal investigation into the healing, and Tierney has already traveled to Vancouver and met the Andersens.

Horgan, an expert on the church's process for canonization, said the inquiry will gather all the medical documentation and seek to interview physicians involved in the treatment. It will take statements from himself and the Andersens.

"It's a rigorous process and the word miracle isn't used. What will be investigated is whether the healing was of such an extraordinary nature as to be medically inexplicable—in other words, something that science can't account for," Horgan said.

If the local investigation is satisfied that is the case, all the material will be sent to Rome to the Vatican's Congregation for the Causes of Saints, the department that investigates candidates for sainthood.

The dossier will be given to a medical consultation team of nine physicians to review, and if they determine the healing to be inexplicable, it then passes to a committee of theologians to see if a connection can be drawn between the medical outcome and Marmion, said Horgan. "If they believe that is the case, it then becomes reviewed by a committee of bishops and if it passes them it is bumped up to the pope. He's the only one who can say it's a miracle," Horgan said.

by Gerry Bellett, *Vancouver Sun,* July 11, 2009

Faith Is Not a Matter of Intelligence

Most people tend to believe only in what they can perceive through their intellect and verify through their senses. They think that reality is limited only to the visible world and do not consider the possibility of a spiritual dimension that exists beyond the physical world.

Maurice Nicoll said, "To act from faith is to act beyond the range of the ideas and reasons that the sense-known side of the world has built in everyone's mind."

David Hawkins said, "It is helpful to remember that neither truth nor enlightenment is something to be found, sought, acquired, gained, or possessed. That which is the Infinite Presence is always present. Moving away the clouds does not cause the sun to shine but merely reveals what was hidden all along. Spiritual work is a commitment and an exploration. The way has been opened by those who have gone before us and set the possibility in consciousness for others to follow."

Enlightenment, therefore, is not necessarily something we can reach or understand through our intellectual abilities. Our intellect helps us to collect the information and knowledge we need in order to be able to feel and experience our faith through our emotional centers.

Application

1- Instead of trying to live this life alone, through the power of your intellect and your abilities only, access the deeper dimensions of spirituality, through prayer and faith so that you can receive direction, assistance, and protection.

2- Take time to grow in awareness of the power of the Spirit and have faith in it. The greater your faith, the greater your power, the greater the guidance and the protection that you are going to experience. "For we walk" Paul said "by faith, not by sight" (2 Corinthians 5:7) In other words, we do not go where we see but where we are guided.

3- Have faith in people and in the goodness of their hearts. There is abundance of goodness and beauty within all of us. Try to get the best out of everybody.

Chapter 4

Ego- The sense of the false center

You are a living magnet. What you attract into your life
is in harmony with your dominant thoughts.

—BRIAN TRACY

What Is the Ego?

The word "ego" is derived from the Greek word meaning "I."
It represents the social part of our self and "who" we think we
are. It is self-generated by conditioning and identifications with
concepts, values, and symbols which become the foundation of our
personality.

The ego is responsible for our self-image, as it is the sum total of
our observed and unobserved thoughts and emotions.

Although egos differ from one person to another, the basic
structure of all egos is exactly the same. Egos, in the sense of the false
center of self, are selfish, defensive, insecure, competitive, aggressive,
fearful, and continually struggling for survival. They suffer from
selective exposure, distorted interpretation, and confusion of opinions
and perceptions with facts. The ego prefers routine over creativity
and it fears the unknown. It continually strives for power and control
over others in order to camouflage its own fears and insecurities

Our Ego Is Unstable

Our ego is neither genuine nor stable. Its self-generated thoughts and emotions are products of its identification with external factors, which themselves are unstable and subject to change at any moment. This identification with unstable factors makes the ego live in continuous fear of change, fear of criticism, of rejection, of loss and death, and makes it cling to power, recognition, and acceptance as its only forms of protection. Consequently, the ego can only experience love as "need and possessiveness," and it only gives in order to receive.

What Are the Effects of the Ego in Us?

The function of the ego is to preserve and satisfy only itself. Its only purpose is to avoid pain and increase pleasure, even through lies and deception. In doing so, and by thinking only of itself first, it initiates in us a vicious circle of subjective chain reactions that direct the state of our mind and consequently our lives. Most of the time, the ego engages the brain to produce thoughts or voices, true or untrue, creating positive or negative emotions in us, as well as verbal or bodily actions which, in their turn, reinforce the ego and its self-created thoughts. Therefore, our ego is the driving force behind our actual behavior, our beliefs and convictions, our bodily reactions, and our psychosomatic illnesses.

A Story

Once upon a time, there was a bird hunter who enjoyed capturing groups of quails by throwing a net over them.

One day the leader of the flock said to the other quails that in order to avoid being captured, next time that the bird hunter throws his nets all over them, they should all put a wing through the net and flap in unison. That way they could all fly away and carry the net with them as well.

When the quails followed the instructions of their leader, they all escaped together, and the hunter was not able to catch any of them for a very long time.

After a while , however, the quails began to argue over their food and hatred set in. No one was prepared any longer, to act as a group but everyone decided to act on their own, driven by their egos, for themselves only.

Well, when the hunter next threw his net over them, they refused to act in unison just to spite each other, allowing the hunter to catch them all.

The Ego Should Be Controlled

In order to free ourselves from the bondages of the ego with all the destructive effects it has on our behavior, mood, and state of health, we must first recognize its existence, its thoughts, its deceptions and its control over us. We must then come to the realization that we are not our egos, we are not our thoughts, we are not our emotions, but we are our pure, real selves that manifest through our bodies and our brains. We are the voice of the inner self, the voice of the super-conscious, the voice of the conscience that the ego is eternally trying to block with its self-justification and convincing thoughts that emanate out of fear, insecurity, jealousy, and competition.

We have to realize that there is no bad person and no one is wrong. It is the overinflated and over-energized ego in some people that blinds them, causing them to act out of selfishness, greed, and hatred. Everybody knows in his heart what is right or wrong. All we have to do is to silence the voice of the ego, to obstruct its delusions of grandeur and persecution, and waken the voice of the soul so that we can achieve an elevated awareness.

Once we achieve this and once we come to the realization that we are all connected to the absolute truth and to each other, then compassion will arise toward everyone and we will consequently be able to spread love and forgiveness around us. This will initiate a chain reaction, which in turn will allow us to receive and enjoy love and forgiveness from others.

Mother Teresa once said, "You and I must come forward and share the joy of loving. But we cannot give what we don't have. That's why we need to pray so that we can see God in each other. And if we see God in each other, we will be able to live in peace."

Only the spiritual realization and the truth of the grace within us can free us from the grip of our ego and enable us to experience an ultimate state of existence of bliss and joy, which some mystics have called the "Christ within" state. Jesus said, "I am the way, and the truth, and the life. No one comes to the Father except through me." (John 14:6) Jesus always referred to our spirit, our indestructible aspect, the soul within us from which all states of eternal, pure love, real joy, and universal peace emanate.

How to Create a Genuine Relationship with Others

Our ego, in its interactions with the egos of other human beings, is responsible for all our emotional hurts, sufferings, reactions, problems, and miseries in this life. A genuine relationship with others can only be created when it is not governed by the ego and the false reality it creates, but on genuine behavior governed by one's real self. Only at this genuine level, beyond the roles and the games of the ego, one can experience unconditional love as opposed to wanting need, consideration instead of dependence, and compassion instead of selfishness.

The further away we move from the ego's grip, the better our relationships become with other people. Our egos separate us from each other, causing suffering, while our spiritual realizations unite us with each other.

This applies very much to another story in which hungry people were sitting around a table filled with plenty of food, but no one could partake in it, as they were all given spoons with very long handles, which they could not maneuver in order to feed themselves.

Eventually, one person suggested that if everyone feeds the person across the table from him, with his long-handled spoon, then they could all eat and satisfy their hunger. The secret was to satisfy the hunger of the other first.

It Is Easy to Get Carried Away

Even religions containing and teaching the ultimate truth fall into the trap of the collective ego and get distorted by thoughts of superiority, leading to criticism of others and creating competition and conflict among the believers. The ego loves to be able to point out the wrongdoings of others, their lack of integrity, their dishonesty, and their lack of consideration for others. Consequently, the message that is passed along is that if someone else is wrong, our individual and collective ego has to be right, it has to be superior, and it has to be judged to be the best.

Application

1- Give up the need to be right.

2- Realize that negative thoughts, together with the created negative emotional energy, can distort your perception of yourself and others, to such an extent that you may act and behave in a completely unreasonable and distorted way. Wars, revolutions, and religious conflicts through the ages are very good examples of such behavior.

3- Untrap your pure consciousness from the bondage of your mind and the dictates of your ego, in order to live happily and in peace.

Chapter 5

Fear

"For God did not give us a spirit of cowardice, but rather
a spirit of power and of love and of self-discipline."

(PAUL- 2 TIMOTHY 1:7)

"Do not fear, for I am with you, do not be afraid, for
I am your God; I will strengthen you, I will help you, I
will uphold you with my victorious right hand "

(ISAIAH 41:10)

What Is Fear?

Fear is one of the most basic human emotions. It has been
programmed into our nervous system and it works like an instinct.
It makes us alert to dangers in situations that make us feel unsafe
or unsure, and it prepares us to deal with them, acting as a warning
signal.

The experience of fear can be mild, medium, or intense. It can
be brief or last long, depending on each particular situation and
each person.

Although fear can be helpful in protecting us from a threatening
situation, it can also be one of the most paralyzing emotions. "The
only thing we have to fear is fear itself—nameless, unreasoning,

unjustified terror which paralyzes needed efforts to convert retreat into advance" (FDR—First Inaugural Address, March 4, 1933).

How Does Fear Work?

When we sense danger, our brain reacts instantly, sending signals that activate our nervous system. This causes physical responses in our bodies, such as a faster heartbeat, rapid breathing, and an increase in blood pressure. The body normally stays in this "fight or flight" situation until the brain receives an "all clear" message and turns off the response.

A Taoist Story Written *by* **Michael Miles** *on* **January 14, 2009 Posted** at *www.pickthebrain.com/blog/life-should-be-effortless*

A man was afraid of his shadow. He desperately wanted to get away from it, so he started running. He ran and ran and ran, but the shadow kept following him. The faster he ran, the faster the shadow went, keeping up with him. When he stopped, to his great surprise and amazement, the shadow was still there, right by his side. He concluded that he hadn't been running fast enough, so he started running again, even faster. Unfortunately, it was too much for his body to endure, and he dropped dead of a heart attack.

As a result of his overwhelming fear, he failed to realize that if he had stood in one spot long enough, his shadow would have disappeared because the sun would have set.

The moral of the story is that it is better to deal with our fears consciously and in a logical manner, instead of trying to run away from them by denying or repressing them. Fears that are realized, observed, and dealt with disappear fast from our lives.

How Can We Deal with Fear?

Fear is simply lack of faith, lack of spiritual realization, and lack of clear understanding of ourselves. As spiritual beings, we have nothing to worry about or fear. When our mind is healthy, it will be capable of keeping a positive attitude under the most devastating circumstances. A mind trained in spirituality and in faith has the courage to face fear and the ability to realize that, somehow, all things work together for the best.

Therefore, we have nothing to fear, be anxious, or worry about. To the contrary, we have everything to praise God for.

"There is no fear in love, but perfect love casts out fear; for fear has to do with punishment, and whoever fears has not reached perfection in love" (John 4:18).

Application

1- Trust in God. "If God is for us, who can be against us?" (Romans 8:31). The answer is "no one."

2- Every time a frightening thought or idea comes into your mind, think of the above quotation, visualize Jesus standing by you and protecting you, and you will see how much easier you can manage your fears and anxieties.

3- Take each day one at a time instead of worrying about how you will cope with the rest of the week or the month or the year. Each day can provide us with new and different ways to deal with our problems, especially if we trust in the power of God.

Chapter 6

Humility

"The greatest among you will be your servant. All who exalt themselves will be humbled, and all who humble themselves will be exalted."

(MATTHEW 23:11-12)

Humility as a virtue is a major theme of both the Old and the New Testament.

Humility is the most important attribute and quality of character for a successful spiritual life. It not only paves the way to God's presence and guidance in one's life, but it requires the development of virtues such as sincerity, honesty, and genuine self-criticism in people. Consequently, humility is what creates peace and harmony between people and what heals old wounds as it allows one to see the dignity and worth of others, to recognize all their positive attributes, and to see the existence of God in everyone. "Do nothing from selfish ambition or conceit, but in humility regard others as better than yourselves." (Philippians 2.3) as "The greedy person stirs up strife, but whoever trusts in the LORD will be enriched." (Proverbs 28:25)

A Story

Philip II (382-336 BC, Macedonian king from 353-336 BC, the father of Alexander the Great) employed two men whose sole responsibility was to address him twice each day, once each morning and once in the evening.

Their morning duty was to say to their king: "Philip, remember that you are but a human," and in the evening to ask him: "Philip, have you remembered that you are but a human?"

What a wonderful wisdom!

Power Comes from God

Apostle Paul writes to the Corinthians in verse 12: 9-10 "But he said to me, 'My grace is sufficient for you, for power is made perfect in weakness.' So, I will boast all the more gladly of my weaknesses, so that the power of Christ may dwell in me. Therefore I am content with weaknesses, insults, hardships, persecutions, and calamities for the sake of Christ; for whenever I am weak, then I am strong."

A humble person knows the evidence and truth of what cannot be perceived by the senses, and he recognizes without doubt that his achievements and successes in life are not due to his own capabilities and intelligence, but that they are all the gifts of God, to whom all praise and glory is due.

What are the attributes of a child?

"He (Jesus) called a child, whom he put among them, and said, 'Truly I tell you, unless you change and become like children, you will never enter the kingdom of heaven. Whoever becomes humble like this child is the greatest in the kingdom of heaven." (Matthew 18:2-4)

The innocence and the pure heart of a child are what we need in order to be reborn in spirit.

The Power of Humility

Humility gives us the strength to transcend the need to be praised or justified by others. "Do not boast about tomorrow, for you do not know what a day may bring. Let another praise you, and not your own mouth— a stranger, and not your own lips." Proverbs (27:1-2)

Humility enables us to cultivate modesty instead of pride, spontaneity instead of hypocrisy, and moderation instead of greed, as peace and love cannot be achieved through arrogance or anger.

Wealth, power, or high positions gained at the expense of others can only bring anxiety, disharmony, and unhappiness.

Criticism and Gossip Hurt Oneself and Others

Criticism, gossip, and lies are great sins that are very hard to correct. They are toxic to the spirit and the greatest obstacles in the path of spirituality. They are based on the ego and on self-pride. They are normally derived by self-perceptions of righteousness or of higher intelligence, greater learning, superior position, more wealth, better looks, etc.

"The good person brings good things out of a good treasure, and the evil person brings evil things out of an evil treasure. I tell you, on the day of judgment you will have to give an account for every careless word you utter; for by your words you will be justified, and by your words you will be condemned." (Matthew 12:35-37)

Application

1- Do not judge, so that you may not be judged. For with the judgment you make you will be judged, and the measure you give will be the measure you get. Why do you see the speck in your neighbor's eye, but do not notice the log in your own eye? Or how can you say to your neighbor, "Let me take the speck out of your eye", while the log is in your own eye? You hypocrite, first take the log out of your own eye, and then you will see clearly to take the speck out of your neighbor's eye. (Matthew 7:1-5)

2- " Do not speak evil against one another, brothers and sisters. Whoever speaks evil against another or judges another, speaks evil against the law and judges the law; but if you judge the law, you are not a doer of the law but a judge." (James 4:11)

3- Be considerate and not be selfish; don't try to impress others. Be humble, thinking of others as better than yourself, as for "God opposes the proud, but gives grace to the humble." (1Pet5: 5)

4- We have to maintain a spiritual dignity by paying attention to what pleases our fellow human beings, as opposed to what pleases ourselves.

"Do nothing from selfish ambition or conceit, but in humility regard others as better than yourselves." (Philippians2-2;3)

Chapter 7

Happiness

Success is not the key to happiness. Happiness is the key to success.

—ALBERT SCHWEITZER

Happiness Is Attainable

My attempts to define and find happiness began as I started my graduate studies in psychology.

Before that, as I dwelled in disciplines like philosophy, anthropology, sociology, and religion, many questions arose in my mind relating to our human existence, to our purpose here on earth, and to the definition of happiness. Why do people want to be happy? And if happiness is so highly valued, what is stopping us from achieving happiness?

I eventually came to realize that the meaning of happiness is different for different people. Not one universally acceptable definition has been given.

Some holistic theorists believe that we feel happiness when our body, mind, and soul are in harmony.

Some people believe that they would be happy if they could either possess money, have power, or have many friends. Others think that they would be happy if they could enjoy different types of pleasure or gain knowledge, gain virtue, and so on. Still others feel that good health is enough to make them happy. One thing is for certain, that whatever we feel we lack, the possession of it seems to be our secret of happiness. We can therefore deduce that happiness would only last for a very short time, until another need or desire develops.

So keeping in mind that we have both biological and psychological needs that differ in importance from person to person, happiness could, very simplistically, be defined as a feeling of well-being, which consequently would be different from one person to another.

What Are the Causes of Unhappiness?

Below are five known causes that lead to unhappiness:

1. Not knowing your true identity
2. Clinging to the idea of permanence in an ever-changing world
3. Fear of change
4. Identifying with the society-induced delusions of the ego
5. Fear of death

Abraham Lincoln, in his statement, "Most folks are about as happy as they make up their minds to be." implied that the pursuit of happiness might be a matter of choice.

What Did the Ancient Greeks Say?

"The most obvious mark of the happy man" said Aristotle, "is that he wants nothing, as the happy life leaves nothing to be desired." Therefore if we train ourselves to have no desires or unfulfilled wishes, we should be happy.

Plato identifies happiness with spiritual well-being, with a state of harmony in the soul, an inner peace that results from the proper order of all the soul's parts.

In Plato's *Republic,* Socrates challenged to show that the just man will be happier than the unjust, even if by all external considerations he seems to be at a disadvantage. He taught that the just person does not permit the several elements within himself to interfere with one another by setting his own inner life in order and by being at peace with himself. Such men are made happy by the possession of justice and temperance, while the miserable ones are made more miserable by the possession of vice.

What Is Nirvana?

Nirvana is a state of mind. As such, it can only be achieved by controlling our mind and our needs, and by eliminating our desires.

A Story

"The Window" (author unknown)

Two men, both seriously ill, were occupying the same hospital room. One man was allowed to sit up in his bed for an hour a day. His bed was next to the room's only window. The other man had to spend all his time flat on his back.

The men talked for hours on end. They spoke of their wives and families, their homes, their jobs, their involvement in the military service, where they had been on vacation. And every afternoon when the man in the bed next to the window could sit up, he would pass the time by describing to his roommate all the things he could see outside the window.

The man in the other bed would live for those one-hour periods when his world would be broadened and enlivened by all the activity and color of the outside world. The window overlooked a park with a lovely lake, the man had said. Ducks and swans played on the water while children sailed their model boats. Lovers walked arm in arm amid flowers of every color of the rainbow. Grand old trees graced the landscape, and a fine view of the city skyline could be seen in the distance. As the man by the window described all this in exquisite detail, the man on the other side of the room would close his eyes and imagine the picturesque scene.

One warm afternoon, the man by the window described a parade passing by. Although the other man could not hear the band, he could see it in his mind's eye as the gentleman by the window portrayed it with descriptive words. Unexpectedly, a strange thought entered his head: *Why should he have all the pleasure of seeing everything while I never get to see anything?* It didn't seem fair. As the thought fermented, the man felt ashamed at first. But as the days passed and he missed seeing more sights, his envy eroded into resentment and soon turned him sour. He began to brood and found himself unable to sleep. He should be by that window—and that thought now controlled his life.

Late one night, as he lay staring at the ceiling, the man by the window began to cough. He was choking on the fluid in his lungs. The other man watched in the dimly lit room as the struggling man by the window groped for the button to call for help. Listening from across the room, he never moved, never pushed his own button, which would have brought the nurse running. In less than five minutes, the coughing and choking stopped, along with the sound of breathing. There was only silence—deathly silence.

The following morning, the day nurse arrived to bring water for their baths. When she found the lifeless body of the man by the window, she was saddened and called the hospital attendant to take it away—no words, no fuss.

As soon as it seemed appropriate, the man asked if he could be moved next to the window. The nurse was happy to make the switch, and after making sure he was comfortable, she left him alone.

Slowly, painfully, he propped himself up on one elbow to take his first look. Finally, he would have the joy of seeing it all himself.

He strained to slowly turn to look out the window beside the bed. It faced a blank wall.

How Can You Achieve Happiness?

The right attitude in life and doing the right thing at all times is a sure way to bring happiness into everyone's life. The right attitude can be achieved not only by a negative legalism but by following the eight jewels of Christianity, the eight principles that Jesus taught during His famous Sermon on the Mount. They are His prescription for a happy living and for experiencing the kingdom of God on earth.

1- "<u>Blessed are the poor in spirit, for theirs is the kingdom of heaven.</u>" (Mathew 5:3)

Blessed are the people who can control their self-centeredness and their vanity, which prevent spiritual development. Only by diminishing our egos, by controlling the overflowing of thoughts and ideas in our minds, and by realizing our inner selves we shall let the power and grace of God flow through us.

To be poor in spirit means to think less and less about the past, the future, and others, and to put God as the first and foremost thought in our minds.

2- "<u>Blessed are those who mourn, for they will be comforted</u>". (Matthew 5:4)

Sickness and disease are lack of harmony between oneself and one's environment. In order for one to enjoy physical, mental, and spiritual health, one must start by mourning for oneself and the death he brought upon himself, so that his real inner self can be awakened through prayer, repentance, and God's forgiveness and grace.

Anytime a spiritual law is broken, consequences follow, in the same manner as when physical or social laws are broken. Human error of judgment, will, or purpose causes bad things to happen. Human selfishness, indifference, and stupidity are always at the root of human misery and suffering.

God comforts His people when bad things happen to them by giving them His peace and by giving them courage, hence alleviating their sorrows.

3- "<u>Blessed are the meek for they will inherit the earth</u>" (Matthew 5:5)

Blessed are the emotionally stable and mature people who have reached such a state of humility and spiritual growth that nothing can disturb their peace of mind. They are neither excitable nor depressed. They are calm, kind, patient, quiet, persistent in their efforts, in control of their emotions, and transparent to anything that goes on around them. To be meek does not mean to think less of yourself but to think more of God and His infinite power over everyone and everything.

4- "<u>Blessed are those who hunger and thirst for righteousness, for they will be filled.</u>" (Matthew 5:6)

Happiness does not lie in success, fame, or power, but in righteousness. It feels good to do good. Real happiness is different than simple excitement. Real happiness brings tears of joy into one's eyes. It is derived from meaning that is related to the virtues of discipline and obedience. They are both necessary for spiritual growth and peace of mind in life.

5- "<u>Blessed are the merciful, for they will receive mercy.</u>" (Matthew 5:7)

When God's goodness can be seen, when His presence is not doubted by the human intellect, His mercy can be experienced by all of us.

Every one of us has received so much mercy from God that we all need to be as merciful as possible to our fellow human beings.

As every action in this universe produces a reaction of equal strength:

1- Treat people nicely and you will be treated nicely.
2- Spread love, compassion, and forgiveness around you and you will encounter love, compassion, and forgiveness.
3- Spread happiness to those around you in order to be happy.
4- Make everyone you meet feel beautiful and unique.
5- Remember, you have to give in order to receive. This is the law of proportionate return and of attraction.

6- "<u>Blessed are the pure in heart for they will see God</u>" (Matthew 5:8)

The pure are the people who have managed to get rid of all negative emotions and feelings like jealousy, anger, hatred and misery out of their lives, and they have adopted a healthy, positive, loving, and compassionate attitude toward all of God's creation.

Being positive breeds positive actions. Emotional and spiritual health enable us to experience the mercy, the grace, and the presence of God in our lives.

Mother Teresa wrote "We all long for heaven, where God is. But we have it in our power to be in heaven with God, right now, at this very moment. To be at home with God means loving the unlovable as He does, helping the helpless as He does, giving to those in need as He does, serving the lonely as He serves, rescuing the perishing as He rescues. This is my Christ. This is the way I live."

7- "Blessed are the peacemakers for they will be called children of God" (Matthew 5-9)

Every one of us can be a peacemaker by doing and saying something positive and by building bridges.

Being a peacemaker can be extremely difficult but rewarding, especially when using the restoring power of love and when bringing Jesus Christ into human hearts.

Peacemakers know how to be at peace with themselves first, and therefore they can live at peace with others and they can make peace for others.

8- "Blessed are those who are persecuted for righteousness sake for theirs is the Kingdom of Heaven." (Matthew 5:10)

Persecution is a situation that many of us have faced or will face in the form of rejection, harassment, peer pressure, wrong assumptions and accusations, or discrimination.

Emotional persecution, which can be a result of envy and jealousy for someone's success, normally attacks both losers and winners. It attacks one's self-esteem and self-image, which often results in self-persecution and experiences of guilt and remorse.

In order for someone to get out of persecution as a winner and not a loser, one needs to be able to remain positive at all times and under any circumstances. He needs to be equipped with a spiritual and emotional support system, to insist on doing what he considers to be the right thing to do, to be forgiving toward those who hurt him, to persist in trusting God, and to pray for strength and endurance.

Application

1- Understand that happiness is the beginning of your journey to your self-fulfillment

2- Enjoy happiness by meditating. When you meditate you are allowing your prefrontal cortex in your brain to release the following natural chemicals, which are linked to happiness:

  a- Serotonin, which is responsible for raising your self-esteem
  b- Oxytocin, which elevates your pleasure hormones
  c- Opiates, which are the natural painkillers of the body
  d- Dopamine, which is an anti-depressant

Chapter 8

Prayer

So I say to you, ask, and it will be given to you; search, and
you will find; knock, and the door will be opened for you. For
everyone who asks receives, and everyone who searches finds,
and for everyone who knocks, the door will be opened.

(LUKE 11: 9-10)

Prayer Is a Powerful Tool

I grew up in a house with a prayer room dedicated to God, filled with icons of Jesus, the Virgin Mary, saints, and angels. I was encouraged to go in there and pray every time I needed to talk to God. I felt as if God and His saints were there waiting for me at all times. My prayers filled me with peace, sometimes with excessive joy and bliss, or with a compassionate heart for all the children in the world who needed my prayer.

Later, when I grew up and started looking for a logical explanation on how things work, I found out that prayer is a thought force which, when focused in the right direction, becomes the most powerful tool a human being can possess. I realized that prayer is the path to communion with God, to mystical experiences, to spiritual development, and to absolute happiness and bliss in life.

I am very sorry to say that, according to my findings, many people have never tasted the beauty of a mystical communication with God and have never experienced the usefulness of prayer. They have never realized that more things are achieved by prayer than the world can even dream of.

The Two Kinds of Prayer

Prayer is of two kinds, the inner or mystical and the outer or obvious. Both kinds help to warm up the heart and the soul of man and to bring him closer to his Creator.

Praying by constantly and unceasingly repeating the Lord's Prayer should take place every day, every hour, even during the busiest times of day, until a bridge is formed between our inner and outer worlds, until harmony is created between us, God, and the others, until our everyday lives and our fate can be influenced positively by our communion with God's divine grace and love. Apostle Paul said "I pray for several hours a day, however, I hope my life is a prayer." Hence we should constantly strive to contact God through continuous prayer, as prayer that only cries out for help in time of emergency can never be compared with the steady outreach for God.

Mystical prayer can also be called meditation. It is the silent, non-verbal, and spiritual form of prayer. It is thinking about God. It can take place at any time and any place, and ideally, it should be a twenty-four-hour affair every day. It can be done while walking, sitting, lying down, or at any time that one wishes to collect one's thoughts and contact God.

It is a matter of habit and training of the mind for every one of us to learn to carry on with our everyday life and commitments, while our soul is always ready to enter the infinite spiritual realm of the cosmos, and our mind is in continuous contact with God.

How Does Prayer Influence Our Lives?

1- Prayer awakens our powers and actualizes our dreams. If we can visualize health, happiness, and prosperity, we will achieve them through our prayers. If we affirm our wishes quietly but strongly and confidently with faith, they will be fulfilled. Jesus Himself, in the gospel of John, promised His disciples that "Whatsoever you ask the Father in my name, will be given to you."

2- Prayer reduces stress and is the best solution for marital and relationship problems. When couples pray together, they grow closer to each other and lead happier married lives.

3- Prayer helps with everything from insomnia to neurosis, and it produces the best physiological responses in ill people.

Herbert Benson, the Harvard Medical School cardiologist, found out that patients who recite prayers, practice meditation, or repeat mantras can reduce stress, lower their metabolic rates, slow their heart rates, and ease their pains. He has also found out that the more "spiritual" people are, the more they are able to get in touch with a presence that is beyond them, yet close to them and, hence, the fewer medical problems they are likely to experience.

According to studies conducted at the University of Wisconsin-Madison by Richard Davidson and his colleagues, brain activity in Tibetan lama monks who are skilled in meditation has shown that the lamas' baseline of brain activity is much further to the left than the activity of people who often have negative thoughts. People who have greater activity in the left prefrontal cortex are believed to be much happier people and to have a better immune system.

What Makes Some Peoples' Prayers More Effective?

I have noticed more than once that some people's prayers are more effective and their secret wishes seem to be answered more often than others. The reason, I concluded, is a combination of their positive attitudes, their low levels of negativity, their pure intentions, clear focus, increased humility, greater compassion, greater forgiveness, a clear and focused mind, a higher degree of mental development, and a practice of prayer aimed at the well-being of everyone.

If our actions are not equal to our prayers, it means that our prayers are just recited but not felt, so there is a greater possibility that they will not be answered.

Realize What You Could Be Missing

Some people who have never tried to pray—people who do not believe in anything except the external world perceived only through their own five senses—will never be able to understand the power of prayer and how much they are missing by not tapping into the universal power in order to be guided and helped by It, through life.

A True Event

Awhile ago, during a United Nations celebration of forty years of being in existence, Mother Teresa, being fully aware of the fact that one of the rules of the United Nations is no prayers, marched to the podium, first prayed, and then said, "You and I must come forward and share the joy of loving. But we cannot give what we don't have. That's why we need to pray so that we can see God in each other. And if we see God in each other, We will be able to live in peace."

Application

1- Believe absolutely in the power of God, expect the gifts of the Spirit, trust that God knows your needs and wishes, and you will see the results of your prayers.

2- Visualize prayer as a ladder to God or a flow of energy that gets directed toward Him, and from there to the whole universe. This energy, which gets released through prayer, performs miracles inside and around you, to an extent that you can never imagine. The more the mind concentrates on prayer, the more it is elevated to a different level of awareness of consciousness. Once you feel the prayer, you can feel the transformation. Once you hear the prayer and let it sink into your being, you can change who you are.

3- Constantly praise God, chanting hymns, reading the Bible, occupying yourself with godly principles and truths, in order to open up a tremendous possibility of success and fulfillment in your life.

4- Remember that God consciousness is a continuous remembrance that God lives in all of us, and act according to that notion, having devotion to God and serving others with humility.

Chapter 9

Meditation

Each of us is now being drawn, in one way or another, to that great vision that comes from beyond the personality. It is more than a vision—it is an emerging force. It is the next step in our evolutionary journey. Humanity, the human species, is longing now to touch that force, to shed that which interferes with clear contact. We are evolving from five-sensory humans into multi-sensory humans. Our five senses together form a single sensory system that is designed to perceive physical reality. The perceptions of a multi-sensory human extend beyond physical reality to the larger dynamical systems of which our physical reality is a part.

—GARY ZUKAV

What Is Meditation?

For many years, I heard people around me talk about meditation but every time I tried to find out more about it, as to exactly what meditation is, how it can be done, and what can be achieved through it, all I got were different versions and different experiences of different people, without any concrete information. Eventually, after I researched the issue further by reading works by Eastern and Western practitioners, I came to the conclusion that meditation is the ability to keep still, sit still, and empty one's mind of every wordly thought, feeling, and emotion while concentrating fully on only one positive, spiritual thought, concept, picture, or object—for as long as required or until realizations are achieved.

Another way of meditating is by repeating the infinite name of God with every breath that one takes until eventually one becomes a living vibration of His name, in absolute union with Him, thus achieving an absolute bliss, an inner calmness, and God's guidance through life's trials and hardships.

Meditation Is a Very Important Tool

Meditation offers both physical, mental, emotional and spiritual benefits to the practitioner.

One of the most basic functions of meditation is that it relaxes us mentally and physically. When we go deeper into meditation:

1. our breath becomes more rhythmic,
2. our blood pressure drops and our heart rate slows down,
3. the prefrontal cortex of our brains gets activated and the release of neurotransmitters like dopamine, serotonin, oxytocin, and other brain opiates are released.

On an emotional and spiritual level meditation is used for the purification of the mind and the realization of our true nature. When we go deeper into ourselves,

1. We reach a state of deeper awareness and understanding and we feel the essence and the presence of God,
2. the emotional fevers of life get reduced, and the insecurities and anxieties in our lives are replaced with hope and faith,
3. Consequently our suffering is eradicated as we see things as they really are, without the distortions that our egos create.

What are the benefits ?

It has been proven repeatedly that those who pray and meditate experience a greater inner peace, an increase of universal love, increased patience and compassion, easier forgiveness, better health, and more confidence that they are guided and protected by God.

In a more spiritual realm, God answers the call of each one of us who meditates in His name. When we vibrate the name of God steadily, every day, every hour, every minute, when God's name becomes so strong in our consciousness that we can feel those vibrations in every part of ourselves, we eventually develop a deep connection with the infinite light of God in which there is just bliss without fears that we cannot conquer and no relationship that we cannot perfect.

Scientific Discoveries

On a physiological realm, Dr. Lily Feng of the Baylor College of Medicine in Houston, Texas, found out that people who are at peace with themselves and who practice regular meditation have cells that survive longer than the cells of people who work for a living. The mind state, she explains, can alter the effects and the expression of the genes and their effects on the body. Dr. Feng also discovered the same results with the cells of the people who had after-death experiences. Their cells survive for eighteen hours longer than the cells of ordinary people. (A pilot study in gene regulation by Mind-Body Interaction Quan-Zhen Li, Ph.D.M.D., 1 Ping Li, PH.D.., 2 Gabriella E.Garcia M.D., 2 Richard J. Johnson, M.D., 2 and Lili Feng,MD2

What Do Other Scientists Say?

In 1992, the neuroscientist Richard Davidson from the University of Wisconsin visited the Himalayas and wired up few monks to learn more about what happens in their brains during meditation

The result of the study with the Buddhist monks showed that meditation results in decreased activity in the parietal lobes, which are located at the top and back of the brain with the result that a person feels that there is no boundary between themselves and the rest of the universe. Also, there appears to be an increased activity in the limbic system, which regulates the production of emotions.

I find this new field of Neurotheology which uses the knowledge of Psychology, Parapsychology and Neuroscience extremely fascinating and important in order to understand the neural activities in the body during religious experiences and altered states of consciousness.

Application

1- Have a silent period of meditation at the beginning of each day in order to receive inspiration and to transform your consciousness to a higher level of awareness, increasing your intuitive levels and experiencing a more virtuous and inspired life, with more compassion and love toward those around you.

2- "Life starts with a breath and ends with a breath" said Yogi Bhajan. In order to meditate successfully, you can start by taking a few deep breaths in order to relax your muscles. You can also chant a hymn. Then place Jesus in the center of our mind, focusing on and identifying with Him, and just keep the feeling of His presence in your mind for as long as possible.

3- By meditating in God's name, by showing devotion to God and getting engaged in acts of compassion, you will be creating a unity between body, mind, and soul, and thus a total harmony inside and outside yourself. This will enable you to get liberated from life's illusions and see the divine spark in the world.

Chapter 10

Mindfulness

I have learned to be happy where I am. I have learned that locked within the moments of each day are all the joys, the peace, the fibers of the cloth we call life. The meaning is in the moment. There is no other way to find it. You feel what you allow yourself to feel, each and every moment of the day.

—RUSS BERRIE

What Is Mindfulness?

The very first time I became aware of the meaning of mindfulness was when I heard a terminally ill friend of ours saying that his main regret in life, now that his life was drawing to an end, was that he had waited very long to "start living."

He meant, as he explained later, that during the richest years of his life, he failed to develop a conscious awareness of being fully present to the joys with which life had blessed him. Life seemed to have passed him by, without giving him the chance to enjoy the wonders of his momentary experiences or to express the love he felt spontaneously and with enthusiasm.

Mindfulness, therefore, is being fully conscious of our bodies. It is of being conscious of every moment that goes by us and every activity, thought, or emotion that we experience during that moment. "The secret of health for both mind and body is not to mourn for the past, worry about the future, or anticipate troubles, but to live in the present moment wisely and earnestly." Buddha said.

Mindfulness is the process of being awake to life, of keeping one's attention focused to one's body, and to the present reality. It is what joins our bodies to the cosmic realm like our personal computer connects us to the Internet. It is the process of getting out of our subjective world to a more objective reality and of experiencing it fully.

These practices, which are all based on attention, and on being aware of the moment, serve to raise our level of awareness, to create a mind of God-consciousness and hence an entirely new perspective of seeing things as they really are objectively, and not as they seem to be.

How Can We Achieve Mindfulness?

One way of achieving mindfulness is by stopping the turmoil of anxiety-provoking thoughts in our minds and by fixing our attention and awareness onto our present state of being or onto a present activity.

If we can concentrate in our breathing as a reminding technique to come back to the present time, we can create a harmonious awareness between body and mind, enabling a healing process to start and for peace and joy to be re-established in our lives.

Most people breathe twenty thousand times in an average day. Rhythmic, abdominal breathing provides us with adequate oxygen necessary to restore the body. As we inhale, we become more energized, and as we exhale, more relaxed.

When breathing becomes also a reminder to us of the present time and of the value of the moment, it does offer us a moment of recollection, rest, and renewal, too.

What Is the Process?

In order to experience the mindfulness process with all its physical, psychological, and spiritual benefits:

1- Start with meditating on God's name or focusing on your breathing.

2- Observe your interfering thoughts and let them go without passing any judgment on them. See what type of thoughts come to your mind, how many, and how fast they go by.

3- Observe your emotions as they develop as a result of your thoughts. Do not attach any label to them, and let them go by. Follow the same procedure irrespective of whether your emotions are happy or unhappy.

4- Observe your bodily sensations. They are the natural consequences of your thoughts and emotions.

5- Accept the moment as it comes, as it is meant to be, and just be in it, as God has made it for us. Be fully alive and alert; live it without any conclusions.

6- Learn to experience each activity in your day with enthusiasm and freshness, as if it is happening for the first time, without comparing the present experience to the past experiences. Comparing means drawing from the references of your memory, hence being a victim of the playing up of your subjective mind. Stop living in an automated manner, experiencing boredom, dullness, fear, and anxiety.

7- Carl Rogers said, "I have learned that my total organism sensing of a situation is more trustworthy than my intellect." Learn to trust your own decisions and intuition concentrating on your gut feelings.

8- Practice "being" rather than "doing" and enjoy every moment of it. You do not have to do anything or go anywhere. It is never necessary to hurry or rush your life away. Learn to watch the minutes go by on the clock. Every moment is precious, as life is precious and very short.

9- Forget the past, forget the people who belonged to your past; they are part of history. Ignore the future, it is the unknown, full of "ifs" and "whens." Concentrate on the present. It is the only thing that you can control and change. "For tomorrow I offer no answers, for yesterday I hold no apologies. This moment is a gift which I honor by fully living in it," Mary-Anna Radmacher-Hershey said.

10- There is a time, a place, and a reason for everything in life, positive or negative. As long as we are fully aware of it, as it is happening, and forget about it when it is done, we can always learn something from it. "Thy will be done" is the appropriate attitude in each instant and the best prayer to be meditating on.

For everything there is a season, and a time for every matter under heaven:
^{2} a time to be born, and a time to die;
a time to plant, and a time to pluck up what is planted;
^{3} a time to kill, and a time to heal;
a time to break down, and a time to build up;
^{4} a time to weep, and a time to laugh;
a time to mourn, and a time to dance;
^{5} a time to throw away stones, and a time to gather stones together;
a time to embrace, and a time to refrain from embracing;
^{6} a time to seek, and a time to lose;
a time to keep, and a time to throw away;

(Ecclesiastes 3 : 1-7)

Mindfulness in Christianity

In Christianity, mindfulness is the devotional practice of remembering at all times that Jesus is constantly within us, guiding us, protecting us and helping us. Christians meditate on Jesus' name by repeating prayers or chants, with or without the use of the rosary.

What Is the Opposite of Mindfulness?

The opposite of mindfulness occurs when we keep thinking of our past life events (which seem like dreams or nightmares that are gone forever), or of our future concerns (which may never get realized), or of the interference and injustices caused by other people in our lives, instead of being aware of the present moment .

"Life is a succession of moments. To live each one is to succeed," Corita Kent said. The present is just the moment that creates our future. Our future and our past depend on our ability to handle the present. If we manage to handle the present moment successfully and effectively, then we are creating a happy past, hence a happy life and a happy future.

What Do We Want to Achieve by Mindfulness?

We are obviously trying to achieve happiness, as happiness is the end to all our efforts in life. The practice of mindfulness or living in the present moment, when practiced steadily and continually, can become a source of happier living in our lives with less stress, less anxiety, and more productivity.

As we learn to pray continually or to concentrate on our breathing and our present activity at every moment of our lives, we can appreciate the fact that we are alive and well, the fact that we are loved and guided, and that there is potential for peace and bliss in this existence.

What Is Stress?

We label as stress the physiological and psychological responses in our bodies that arise as a result of pleasant or unpleasant events or thoughts in our lives.

Unfortunately, millions of people suffer from unnecessary stress daily, due to a multiplicity of problems and all sorts of difficulties that follow one another each day. These continuous unpleasant and stressful experiences make our lives difficult, sometimes even impossible to enjoy, as our body is pulled into a state of emergency, which leads to disharmony, hence disease.

We all know that some events are more stressful than others, as they preoccupy our thoughts for much longer, creating all sorts of exaggerated feelings and emotions in us.

Fortunately or unfortunately, our life is perceived by our minds not as series of events but as series of experiences.

Experiences are created as a result of our interpretation of outside events. Therefore, we can control, to a great extent, our interpretation of outside events and our responses to them, while it is impossible to control or influence the outside events, as such. The key, therefore, to a stress-free existence is based in our subjective interpretation of the outside events and in our response to them. Hence, a controlled response brings peace to our life and causes much less stress.

The Greek philosopher Epictetus said, "Man is not disturbed by events but the view he takes of them." Therefore, interpreting our experiences as happy ones will make us lead a happy life, while interpreting them as unhappy experiences will result in us having an unhappy life for which we will be the only ones to blame.

How Can We Reduce Stress?

Self-observation and practicing mindfulness can considerably change our negative interpretations, reducing stress and its harmful consequences.

Application

1- Remember that all pain starts and grows from your thoughts when your mind:

       a- feels stressed
       b- gets distracted
       c- is worrying
       d- is defending its values
       e- is thinking about the future
       f- is occupying itself with old memories

2- What starts as a simple thought should not be allowed to be followed by negative emotions and feelings or by physiological and psychological effects that will affect your life causing bodily and mental harm.

3- Become mindful as soon as an unpleasant, exaggerated thought arises, by replacing it with a positive thought and by practicing prayer and meditation techniques in order to stop and divert all future negative mental and bodily effects right there and then.

4- Remember that pain and hurt in this life may be inevitable, but suffering is optional and a matter of choice for you.

Chapter 11

Living a Life of Holiness and Righteousness

We are not human beings trying to be spiritual. We are spiritual beings trying to be human.

—JACQUELYN SMALL

A Story about a Saint and a Scorpion

Once there was a holy man. He used to go every morning to the river nearby for his daily ablution and meditation session.

One rainy morning as usual, he went back to the river again. After bathing, he sat on the edge of the river, ready to start his meditation session, when he saw a good-sized scorpion battling for its life near the edge of the water.

The holy man rushed near the scorpion, picking him up with his bare hands. While he was transporting him to safety, he got stung by the scorpion in his hand. The pain was so great that the man let the scorpion fall back into the water again.

As the holy man sat by the side of the river for the second time, again he saw the struggling scorpion, again he rushed to his rescue, and again he got stung. And again he let the scorpion fall back to the water. The same story was repeated, over and over and over.

A passerby, who happened to be watching, could not help but ask the man why he was trying to save the scorpion that was stinging him every time and why he did not let him drown. To that remark, the holy man answered, "Because it is in the nature of the scorpion to sting, and it is in my nature to help those who are in pain and need my help. It is not easy for any one of us to change his nature."

How Can We Live a Life of Holiness?

Although we do not have to do great things or be missionaries going to far-off lands in order to serve God and to live a "life of holiness," we cannot stay passive either.

To stand still is to die spiritually and to miss out on the life that God is offering us. To stand still means not to stretch ourselves beyond our personal goals and not to look for something deeper, something that will connect us to God and to the needs of other people.

What Did Jesus Say?

Let us go back to what Jesus has taught us. He said to us:

- to love one another, John 13:3
- do to others as you would have them do to you, Mathew 7:12
- to love our enemies, Luke 6:27
- to pray for those who abuse you, Luke 6:22
- to be merciful, Mathew 5:7
- not to be hypocrites, Mathew 6:5-6
- to be righteous, Mathew 5:10
- to forgive, Mathew 5 14,15
- to have clear hearts, Mathew 5:8

and He promised to us that if we practice these things, the grace of God will come upon us.

Therefore, only if we live our life from a spiritual perspective and through the intelligent application of the essence of Jesus' words and teachings, we can realize our path in this life and achieve an elevated awareness.

What Is Our Path in this Life?

Our path is to serve this humanity in light and in peace, with a consciousness of self-realization, and it is to understand clearly the psyche of everyone and everything. By doing so, we can become a "God-realized person" and move into a future that is generous, open, noble, holy, and centered on God and our neighbors.

What Is an Elevated Awareness?

When the true essence of Jesus' teachings enters into our heart and in our everyday actions and deeds, that is called *Christ awareness.* When our word is true and truth prevails in our everyday lives, then we live in our highest consciousness. When we attain this higher consciousness of awareness, we are blessed. To the contrary, when we fight the will of God, nothing happens; everything comes to a standstill, as life is a flow directed by God.

Eckhart Tolle said, "One thing we know: life will give you whatever experience is most helpful for the evolution of your consciousness. How do you know that this is the experience you need? Because this is the experience you are having at this moment."

We cannot fight the general flow of things or we will end up fighting with ourselves and others. When we fight with each other, we become harmful and deceptive to ourselves and to others. Fighting erodes the strength of humanity. It erodes the strength of the individual to live a life of purity of consciousness and in the purity of the light. Intolerance creates a division between each one of us, and our falseness creates a duality.

If we live in untruth, we are separated from God. God is at a distance or is nowhere at all. If we cannot experience God in our life, if we do not feel the spirituality and the light, it means that our egos have taken over, that our distance from our real selves and from our God has widened, our connection has broken down, our prayers do not get answered, and we live a life of struggle and misfortune.

Application

1- Learn to exist in the domain of "being," rather than "doing."

2- Live walking a path of truth and righteousness, praising God, surrendering to God's will, trusting in the words of Jesus, living according to His teachings.

3- Be kind and sharing, be humble and graceful, and you will see that your prayers will be answered and you will attain the peace of life that leads to the liberation of the soul and to the love and grace of God.

4- Take the first step toward this direction: match your deeds with your words, in order to experience the patience, humility, and thoughtfulness toward others that God will supply you with, in order for you to do the work that He requires of you.

5- Start by accepting that whatever happens in your life, it is always for your best. Learn to cooperate with what God wants for you, in order to begin to experience a new sense of connectedness to the Creative Power of all, a deeper relationship with the divine, and an experience of the universal intelligence guiding you through each step of the way.

Chapter 12

Mind and Awareness

"You are today where your thoughts have brought you; you will be tomorrow where your thoughts take you."

—JAMES ALLEN

In my small way and in all humility, I wish to say that I have tried all my life to keep in my mind the kind of thoughts that I wanted to control my life and my actions. I have tried to base my life on honesty, enthusiasm, spontaneity, compassion, and love. I have tried to do the right thing at all times, but I must confess that at times, I failed greatly.

What Are Our Thoughts?

Henry David Thoreau once said, "As a single footstep will not make a path on the earth, so a single thought will not make a pathway in the mind. To make a deep physical path, we walk again and again. To make a deep mental path, we must think over and over the kind of thoughts we wish to dominate our lives."

Our universe is a huge field of energy. We all are systems of energy fields that interact with each other and with the environment at large. The rate at which we relate to this energy field around us determines our life experiences.

Everything in nature is made up of vibrations of energy. Our thoughts are made up of exactly the same vibration of energy, and hence they are the forces with which we build our world. They are the creative building material that shapes our past, present, and future lives, according to their nature. So, consequently, the quality of our life is a function of the quality of our thoughts and of the level of our awareness. If we do not learn how to control our thoughts, we become products and prisoners of our own minds and of the world surrounding us.

What Is Awareness?

Awareness is a perception of the mind, and it cannot exist without the mind. The events that we experience in our minds as dreams when we are sleeping are very similar to the experiences we have when we are awake, as they are both appearances to our minds, totally dependent on our minds, causing the same bodily effects on us.

One of the main differences is that dreams are on the subconscious level, while life experiences are on the conscious level of the mind. The dreams exist while we are sleeping, and the actual life experiences exist while we are awake. They are both different types and levels of awareness.

Whatever exists only as an awareness to the mind, is deceptive and it does not have a real existence; it is transitory. In other words, it is what we call an illusion.

Anne Wilson Schaef said, "We live in a system built on illusions, and when we put forth our own perceptions, we're told we don't understand reality. When reality is an illusion and illusion is our reality, it's no wonder we feel crazy."

Socrates' Famous Story, Written by Plato

A number of men are chained in a dark cave. A fire blazes around them, producing fearful shadows. Falsely assuming that the shadows are real, the prisoners cringe in terror and fear.

One prisoner gets tired of it all. Courageously, he escapes, fights his way through the darkness, and emerges into the sunlight of the real world. He finds himself free.

What happens if he goes back to tell the others of his discovery? If he explains that their pain is only the result of their illusions, will they believe that an entirely new world exists on the outside? Will they welcome his message? Most probably, they will not! Why should they give up their assumptions that they already know what is real? No, they call him a fool and remain in despair.

The Power of Our Minds

Some people are not aware of their subconscious thinking and the power of their subconscious mind. They do not realize that their thinking is what directs their lives accordingly.

Pythagoras said, "One mind runs through the universe." According to quantum physics, your thoughts, beliefs and perceptions concerning any and every event, condition or circumstance determine how Your life experience will unfold in the physical world. (The quantum Gods by Jeff Love,1976)

According to the law of attraction, when you think of something that you really wish for, if you focus on it and if you charge it with the right vibrating energy of feelings and emotion, then you create a sort of magnetic field that attracts to you everything in the universe that is in harmony with your thoughts.

Negative Thoughts

Negative thoughts affect our mental, emotional, and physical health. They drop our body resistance, and they result in sickness.

Emotions such as anger, fear, hatred, bitterness, and envy should have no room in our hearts and minds because they create disastrous results to our health and to our lives. Negative thoughts and emotions first affect the person who creates them and then everybody else around. They serve no purpose, and they have no other function than to create unhappiness, misery, and loss of powerful energy. They cause useless suffering, destroying one's valuable peace of mind, without any benefit to anybody. For nobody's sake must one allow oneself to get ever into that state of mind .

The best way to fight negativity is by becoming positive. A negative attitude met by a positive gets canceled; met by another negative, it becomes complemented and it doubles up.

The best and quickest way to get rid of one's negativity and to get back to one's beautiful, bright, positive mood is by praying and by thinking about one's real self and about God within, the ultimate source of positive energy, health, happiness, and love.

We Create the Negative Emotions

One of the worst illusions we have is that negative emotions are produced by external circumstances, whereas all negative emotions are in us, inside us. This is a very important point. We always think negative emotions are produced by the fault of other people or by the fault of circumstances. Our negative emotions are in ourselves and are produced solely by ourselves.

There is absolutely not a single reason why somebody else's action or some circumstance should produce a negative emotion in us. Remember that no negative emotion can be produced by external causes if we do not allow it. We may not be able to control what is happening around us, but we can definitely control fully what is happening within us.

The Two Realities

We are living simultaneously in two different realities: the outside, which is the reality of the world we are living in, and the inside, which is the reality of our thoughts, beliefs, emotions, and reactions.

People who get completely trapped in the outside reality and let it become their only reality and their only level of awareness get totally controlled by it.

The Conscious Mind

The conscious mind is in the continuous activity of thinking, perceiving, and conceiving. It often lies to us and tricks us. It makes us see reality through the lens of our perception, which is a distorted lens, perceiving reality only through one level of awareness. This awareness is based on our cultural values and belief system and on our preconceived ideas based on our upbringing and on the experiences we have of the outer world.

The only way to control our conscious mind from tricking us with the uncontrollable flow of thoughts and ideas is to start observing the games it is playing on us. In other words, to observe the different continuous thoughts that are passing through our minds and their physiological and psychological effects on us. We can then try to block what is an undesirable, hurting, agitating, and negative thought by replacing it with a positive, promising, joyful thought. By doing that, we start eliminating negative effects on our bodies, our lives, and our environments, and we then start replacing them with positive effects.

How to Control Our Thoughts

Negative thoughts only have an effect on us when we react to them. The minute any particular thought comes into our mind, if we have the ability to classify it as desirable or undesirable and react to it accordingly, we can then be proud that we know how to control our minds, thoughts, emotions, and lives.

Understanding, controlling, and directing our minds in an orderly way is the only way to a happy life and a solution to unhappy thoughts and depressed moods. If we worry or are stressed or troubled in life, it is because we have not learned to control our minds.

Changing our life experience is not about changing the world around us, but changing our perception of the world and being able to see what we want to see.

Our Subconscious Mind

Our subconscious mind is where our experiences, our values, our talents, our feelings and emotions, and everything else are stored in. Depending on its contents, our subconscious mind controls the way that we perceive our outer world through our conscious mind.

Life is perceived not as a series of events but as a series of experiences. Experiences start as thoughts in our minds and then become actions. Therefore, if we control our thoughts, we will be controlling our attitudes, our actions, our experiences, and subsequently the quality of our lives, happy or unhappy.

By controlling our thoughts, our actions, and our visualizations, we become the masters of our destiny, liberated from suffering. Positive visualizations of the ideal states of being lead to a wonderful adventure through life in which we have full control and mastery of what is happening to us and around us.

Tolstoy said, "everyone thinks of changing the world; no one thinks of changing themselves." That is where the problem starts.

Application

1- You are all blessed with your sound minds, which is perfect equipment in order to achieve spiritual development. All you have to do is develop your brains in order to reach the next level of mind awareness.

2- Your entire life is nothing more than a bundle of thoughts and emotions, rather than events. Because you experience what you anticipate and because your life experiences correspond to the quality of your thinking, by entertaining more uplifting thoughts, you can choose to enjoy life, fully realizing that your mind creates its own world for you to live in, depending on the thoughts you are feeding it with.

Chapter 13

God, the Universal power

" Blessed be the pure in heart for they will see God"

(MATTHEW 5:8)

"Whoever does not love does not know God, for God is love."

(1 JOHN: 8)

The Realization of God Is in the Soul

I am very proud and honored to admit that I have always believed, since my early childhood, that I have a special relationship with Jesus Christ. I have felt many, many times during unprecedented difficult situations in my life the presence, the guidance, the blessings, and the mercy of the divine.

According to Albert Einstein's theories and findings, there is a definite plan and design to this creation. Albert Einstein declared that there has to be a certain intelligence behind such a complex and intricate design. "I believe," he said, "that there is a divine intelligent designer behind all that we see in front of us and He has designed a plan for all of us."

The realization of the existence of God manifests itself in people either as power and intelligence or in spiritual terms as wisdom, love, and truth. Each one of us individualizes the expression of this infinite power according to his or her own level of spiritual understanding.

The Idea of God in Ancient Greece

When Plato and Aristotle spoke of God in the *Nicomachean Ethics,* they were not referring to the Olympian gods, for example Zeus, Hera, Athena, Poseidon, etc. The Olympian gods of their times, being already in their second generation, were considered to be manlike creatures, subject to changes, having humanlike passions and desires, making the same mistakes as them; their laws being neither everlasting nor self-subsistent but contingent on other factors. Therefore they were rather considered to be also creations, created by a more superior Creator.

It is evident that for Aristotle and Plato, God is the one who is beyond the universe, the transcendent, the perfectly self-subsistent being, the "uncaused cause," the eternal and the omnipotent. For Plato, the whole cosmos is a theophany, in other words a manifestation of the divine presence, the divine order, and the divine power.

Talking in the deepest Christian terms, we can call it "the Logos," the Word of God, a term which in itself clearly suggests the idea of the cosmos being perceived as a theophany or a self-revelation of God. St. Paul wrote the following, to the Romans: "Ever since the creation of the world His eternal power and divine nature, invisible though they are, have been understood and seen through the things he has made. So they are without excuse;" (Romans 1:20)

The Idea of God

We can therefore see that the idea of God did not generate out of fear in man, as many people believe it to be. If anything, fear is a negative emotion; it creates negative feelings that move us away from God. The idea of God was clearly generated out of deep philosophical thinking, transcendent perception, absolute reasoning, and deductible evidence.

God Is an Omnipotent Force that Works for You

"The kingdom of heavens within," means that in every human being, beneath one's personality, beneath one's ego, behind the roles one plays in society and the masks one wears, exists a completely different self that is part of the infinite power of the universe.

It is this self, this divine spark, that every one of us has inside him, which manifests as a deep subconscious urge, in us, that pushes us to turn to God and to make a conscious union with our Creator, just like a magnetic needle of the compass which always turns to the North Pole.

When we, as human beings, become consciously aware of this power inside us, we actually activate God's omnipotent and creative powers to start working, creating and ruling on our behalf and for our benefit.

Pythagoras said, "One mind runs through the universe." Every act, every move, every thought in our everyday lives done in the name of God and out of our spiritual awareness, produces and activates some great laws and forces that make a huge difference in our lives and in the world.

We Cannot Understand God through Our Intellect

Apostle Paul wrote: "See to it that no one takes you captive through philosophy and empty deceit, according to human tradition, according to the elemental spirits of the universe, and not according to Christ." (Colossians 2:8)

Never try to understand the existence of God through your intellect or try to interpret everything by using your own logic. It is a futile and useless effort, leading only to confusion. A finite mind cannot grasp the infinite. We can learn much more about God by a devotional attitude and by a humble worship, rather than by any amount of mental power.

God Is Contacted Through Prayer

The best way to contact God is through praying, through meditating in silence, in humility, in goodness, and especially in absolute love and compassion.

Only as we turn from the outer to the inner self and to the silence of the within can we hope to make a conscious union with God, to become one with His power and to realize that His power is available for us to use at all times.

The one who makes the connection with the Father in secret and in deepest silence, through mental prayer and deep devotion, will create the right conditions for the grace of God to reach him and for His power to flow through him in order to fulfill his every need.

Know Thyself

The discovery of our real and true self leads us to the intimacy with God, to the realization of God's presence in our lives and to the experience of God's touch, which is accompanied by a sense of warmth, peace, and confidence.

John Calvin said, "If you want to know God, come to know yourself, and if you want to know yourself, come to know God."

Searching for God in the brain

David Biello comments in the October 2007 issue of *Scientific American Mind* on the findings of neuroscientist Mario Beauregard of the University of Montreal and he says that now, we have a new place to look into in order to satisfy our spiritual inquiries and this is located inside our brains. We can now use, FMRI to see what happens inside our brains when we have mystical experiences during prayer and meditation.

The question always remains the same "Is there a God spot in the brain?"

If the answer is "yes" then the new science of Neurotheology will be developed which will reveal the neural correlates of the divine and it will reconcile science and religion together .

Application

In order for Divine Grace to come to you, you must:

1- Get into a personal relationship with God by filling up your heart with the love for God originating from inner gratitude and by continuous prayer.

2- Purify your soul and submit your mind completely to the divine grace, by praying continually, by reading a section from the New

Testament every day, by fasting, and by becoming conscious of your need for God's mercy.

3- Next, you need to increase your accessibility to God. When you feel happy, you should praise God. When you go through difficulties, you should look for God. In your quiet moments, you should worship God. In hard times, you should trust God, and at all times, you should continually thank God. Praising God and thanking God is the greatest weapon you can possess. When you have God, you have everything and you lack nothing. God is your helper, your protector, your provider, your friend, your support and your guide. "… for apart from me, you can do nothing" (John15:5).

4- Forget your senses; they are only made for your physical existence here on earth. Forget your ego; it is the base of your earthly personality, guided by self-interest, by self-love and survival needs, on this Earth and in this society.

5- Trust the divine plan. If something that is happening to you does not seem right at the moment, face it with patience, positive thinking, and humility; consider it a "blessing in disguise" and accept it fully and gracefully, waiting patiently to understand what God's plan is for you. When you do that, you will allow the grace of God to help you cope with the situation.

6- Christ must somehow be touched by our love, by our kindness, devotion, and humility. Only then will He give us his grace. "God opposes the proud, but gives grace to the humble." (1Pet5: 5)

Chapter 14

Mysticism

And he said to them, "To you has been given the secret of the kingdom of God, but for those outside, everything comes in parables;"

(MARK 4:11)

I have always been fascinated by the idea of apprehending the Universe in a much deeper way. I was extremely amazed from a very young age, with the idea that there is the possibility of a more perfect knowledge of God in this life, through which the soul, by the very special grace, is able to contemplate directly the mysteries of the divine presence. I could visualize the mind acting like a tiny transformer scaling down the energy of the universe to the human level of awareness.

I then came across such concepts as "θεωσις" (theosis, translated as becoming one with God) and "μυστικη ενωσις" (translated as mystical union) with God when I started reading the teachings of the esoteric Christianity found in the Philokalia, in the writings of the desert fathers of the third and fourth centuries, and in the writings of St. John of the Cross (1542–1591).

In recent years, I read that a Gallup poll showed that 70 percent of Americans admitted that they have had very unusual and impressive inner mystical experiences in their lifetimes which they did not tell others.

What Is Mysticism?

Mysticism, derived from the Greek word "μυστικός" (mystikos), is the search of the intimate union of the human soul with the divine for the purpose of achieving a direct consciousness of God and experiencing the loving knowledge of the truth of God.

It is the developing of one's personal relationship and communion with God by reaching a higher level of conscious awareness which cannot be reached by either wordly perception or conception, or by any other knowledge.

The aim of practicing mysticism is the inner transformation of a person until he becomes the temple of the Holy Spirit. In the Bible, this is known as the experience of revelation.

Mysticism in Christianity

In the four gospels and the Revelation of the New Testament, the esoteric ideas occupy the predominant place. The four gospels are written for the few, for the ones who have some knowledge of esoteric teachings. "And he said to them, "To you has been given the secret of the kingdom of God, but for those outside, everything comes in parables;" (Mark 4:11)

The mystical part in Christianity is called esoteric Christianity, as opposed to the *exoteric* Christianity, which deals with the standard dogmas and catechism.

The mystic, as opposed to the ordinary Christian who occupies himself with dogmas and catechism, starts from his inner, positive, individual experience of the divine, in which he finds himself as the eternal being.

The development of a mystical life should be the normal outcome in the life of every Christian who prays, as it is the natural result of faith, hope, and charity, and the gifts of the Holy Spirit that every Christian deserves as his or her baptismal rights.

Paul's Account of a Mystical Experience

Apostle Paul wrote the following to the Corinthians: "I know a person in Christ who fourteen years ago was caught up to the third heaven—whether in the body or out of the body I do not know;

God knows. And I know that such a person—whether in the body or out of the body I do not know; God knows— was caught up into Paradise and heard things that are not to be told, that no mortal is permitted to repeat." (2 Corinthians 12:2-4)

What Do the Great Masters Teach Us?

In the Philokalia, the great masters of orthodox Christianity teach us how to develop our inner powers in order to achieve free, direct, and blissful access to the mystery and power that we call God and who responds to us individually.

Critical and central to this mystical development in our Christian lives is our ability to develop inner attention.

What is Inner Attention?

Inner attention is one's ability to watch every thought that goes through one's mind and to try to remain unaffected by it, by being nonjudgmental, while practicing love and repeating prayers and while concentrating all one's energy onto the one focal point of remembering Jesus instead of wasting the power of one's thoughts on trivial things.

This state is mentioned by Paul in his epistle to the Galatians (2:18–21): "But if I build up again the very things that I once tore down, then I demonstrate that I am a transgressor. For through the law I died to the law, so that I might live to God. I have been crucified with Christ; and it is no longer I who live, but it is Christ who lives in me. And the life I now live in the fl esh I live by faith in the Son of God, who loved me and gave himself for me. I do not nullify the grace of God; for if justification comes through the law, then Christ died for nothing".

What Is the Purpose of Inner Attention?

Ordinary life preoccupations in our daily business and inferior impulses render us only partially conscious or half-asleep or unaware of higher levels of consciousness.

Inner attention to a higher reality through continual prayer—as opposed to responding automatically to external stimuli only or to our internal emotions—is the only means to spiritual awakening, to the inflow of a higher power and access to the Holy Spirit, and to the development of the Christ consciousness, "and it is no longer I who live, but it is Christ who lives in me." (Gal.2:20)

What is the Kingdom of Heaven?

The inner transformation that results in us by the intimacy created between us and the Holy Spirit through Jesus Christ is the only way to the higher dimension called the kingdom of heavens or life eternal.

Mystical Experiences During Meditation

People who have been practicing meditation for a long time profess that when we learn to meditate correctly and manage to reach a state of deep concentration, different kinds of sounds are heard in our ears like the sounds of a church bell, and different colored lights manifest within our forehead, in between our two eyebrows. In the beginning, the light starts as a tiny little white bright light. Although white and yellow lights are the most commonly experienced, one may notice, when the eyes are closed, different colored lights as red, blue, green even mixed lights flashing.

After some months of steady and correct meditation, the size of the light increases and one is able to see a full blaze of white light, bigger than the sun. Also the duration and the stability of these sights increase with practice.

These experiences denote that one is transcending the physical consciousness.

What Has Science Discovered?

I was amazed when I heard on TV on the Discovery Channel that neuroscientists who used the tools of psychology and neuroscience in order to probe the neural underpinnings of religious experiences in spiritually active people had identified a network of brain regions that get activated when people feel the presence of God in their lives.

The research was conducted by Dr. Mario Beauregard and Mr. Vincent Paquette, his doctoral student, at the University of Montreal. They tried to discover the brain activity that takes place in the brain of religious people during times of prayer and meditation and while they were having sensations of being in union with God.

They conducted the experiment with fifteen nuns from the Carmelite monasteries in Canada, for six years, in order to measure the electrical activity in their brains.

They started by using an electroencephalogram (EEG) on the nuns when they relived *"unio mystica"* in their memories. Then they used magnetic imaging, (fMRI), to take a picture of their brains during the experience, and thirdly, they injected the nuns with a low-level radioactive chemical for a PET (positron emission tomography) scan in order to measure the levels of the neurotransmitter serotonin in different parts of their brain.

The researchers then reported in the *Neuroscience Letters,* that they found a collection of brain areas that were more active during the recollected mystical experience, and that the caudate nucleus, which is associated with positive feelings such as happiness and bliss, appeared more active during the mystical memories.

"We are seeing things we don't normally see," says Marc Pouliot, an engineer who is analyzing the EEG results

"………………………………………….The two nuns experienced intense bursts of alpha waves in the brains, common in a reflective and relaxed state such as meditation. They also had intense activity in the left occipital region at the back of the brain – which is not what the scientists were expecting in the wake of research by Michael Persinger, a controversial researcher at Laurentian University in Sudbury, who has developed the so-called God helmet. He uses the device to stimulate the right side of the brain, including the parietal lobe, with low-level electromagnetic radiation. In 80 percent of subjects, this induces the sensation that there is a presence in the room. Many weep and say they feel God nearby. However, the real "God experience" may be different, according to the nuns. Rather than crying, they say they felt intense joy and looked forward to the lab experience, since there is little chance they will ever enjoy a true mystical union with God again. "That feeling of peace flowing through you—pacification—tells you He has been here."

Extracts from "Neural Correlates of a Mystical Experience in Carmelite Nuns, by M. Beauregard and V. Paquette, in *Neuroscience*

Letters, Vol. 405, No. 3; 2006. Reproduced with permission of Elsevier "Mystical Hot Spots": In a 2006 study, the recall by nuns of communion with God invigorated the brain's caudate nucleus, insula, inferior parietal lobe (IPL), and medial orbitofrontal cortex (MOFC), among other brain regions. "Reported by *Anne McIlroy, the Globe and Mail's science reporter*

What Stops People from Achieving a Mystical Union?

What stands between us and our inner development is our false sense of our ego. Our ego belongs to the social level of consciousness or the lowest dimension of existence. Eckhart Tolle says that because the ego is compulsively self-centered and hyperactive, the individuals who are driven exclusively by their egos are psychologically insane.

The spiritual goal of most teachings is the minimization of the ego and the experiencing of the self-knowledge and of the true nature of the human being. As long as our thinking remains the same, as long as we use self-justification and negativity, we remain the slaves of our egos.

What Are the Spiritual Benefits of Practicing Mysticism?

The purpose of esoteric Christianity is to take us beyond the level of the individual ego, to awaken our minds, and to help us develop another higher quality of awareness.

When the ego is submissive to the soul, then the soul is in harmony with itself, with the world around it, and with God. In this way, it is freed from the tyranny of the ego and the chaotic state of the mind.

What Are the Results in Us?

When we practice mysticism:

1- Potential forces, abilities, and talents become awakened in us, as we realize that we are a greater person than we have ever imagined ourselves to be.

2- We grow, develop, and expand our inner selves and feel our special relationship to life and others. The separation we feel from each other, which is due to our egos, disappears.

3- Wakening our spirituality leads us to greater compassion and better service toward our fellow human beings.

What Are the Privileges of the Next Level of Mind Awareness?

Once one has achieved spiritual development, nothing is ever the same. He lives beyond his normal conditioned human self.

1. His perceived reality changes, as it is perceived not through logic any longer but through the world of emotions, feelings, love, and compassion.
2. He is more loving, more compassionate, more caring, and on his way for the next levels of mind awareness.
3. His attention becomes awakened as he moves away from his ego and the false sense of self, away from his personal, angry, complaining, stressful, guilty thoughts towards a peaceful powerful mind, sensitive to the needs of others.
4. The best quality of life, the wonderful inner joy, the so-much-desired peace of mind, and the utmost happiness is enjoyed much more by spiritual people, by the people who have realized that there is more to this life than that what the eyes can see, the hands can touch, and the ears can hear.

Application

1. Remember that all esotericism begins with the faith that there is something higher that lies beyond what our senses can perceive and with the effort to connect with it.
2. Recognize the existence of the soul, listen to that inner voice, and accept the notion that something higher that transcends everything else exists in you.

3. Combine this higher knowledge with personal inner work in order to experience a greater life, in which unwanted events no longer happen to you, as you are in control of your inner state.

4. Become aware that your true being is connected to all that exists. Elevate yourself beyond the level of sensuality and turn your soul toward the infinite love and power.

5. Tap on the enormous powers that exist in the universe as well as in yourself.

6. Experience a spiritual life that has less worry, less stress, and less frustration through the process of your inner transformation.

7. Enjoy heavenly bliss, happiness, joy, and the kingdom of God on Earth.

Chapter 15

Death

The real issue is not so much as us getting into
heaven as it is heaven getting into us.

—RICHARD FORSTER

Death which is an irreversible process in our lives, can be, for some people, the most painful, mysterious, fearful and traumatic event, ever experienced.

During the past few weeks, I have been talking daily with someone who was very ill and very close to death. Whenever I come face to face with death, I cannot help but remember my own losses. I think of my father's and my mother's death, and I relive my experiences of loss and grief. I also think of those around me, whose death I may face one day, as well as my own death.

Admittedly, I find all these thoughts very anxious and very fearful. I have discovered, though, that the only secret to living successfully through grief and to achieving the necessary peace to handle thoughts of one's own inevitable death comes with faith. Only faith can give us the strength to endure the most devastating losses.

Apostle Paul refers to death as "The last enemy to be destroyed" in his first epistle to the Corinthians (1 Corinthians 15:26).

But is death the end of our human existence and of our own consciousness, or do we continue to exist in some other place or state of being? Are we immortal souls? Do we experience a place of everlasting reward or eternal torment? Are we conscious after we die? Will we ever meet up with our loved ones again?

What Do People Think of Death?

Most people avoid altogether the thought that one day, sooner or later, they will have to face the inevitability of death. They are scared of the idea of abandoning their much-cherished body. This idea becomes even more unbearable to the individuals who feel that there is nothing after death and that the grave is the end not only of their earthly existence but of their existence altogether.

Many people who have experienced a momentary death experience as a result of an accident or out of complications on an operating table have given the account of seeing a very bright white light.

Physicists say that this light is the field of undifferentiated energy from which all matter—and therefore all thought—emerges mysteriously and breaks down into it again at the end. If that is correct, there is nothing to fear of death, as death seems to be not a "nothingness" but an "everything-ness."

A Life Story

I was speaking to a friend of mine who had a near death experience but she was eventually revived, during the birth of her first child.

She described it as a very serene and peaceful experience. She said that it felt as if she was walking up a beautiful green hill. Although the hill was steep, it required absolutely no effort to climb it.

She said that she looked at her body but what she saw was a colorless sensation of the self without any concrete boundaries. Almost a blurred sense of the self and the space around it. Yet everything else seemed to be colorful, the green grass, the blue sky and the white light........

Am I dead? she wondered. Can death be such a sense of well being with no darkness and no fear ? Everyting seemed so familiar around her as if she had been there before.

She then realized that she was not alone. They were presences around her. Nobody was speaking to anybody else but a very positive, safe and loving sensation surrounded all.

She opened her eyes, she felt the excruciating pain in her abdomen, she was lying on the operating table with anxious faces all over her body, trying their very best, to bring her back to life.

Death Is Not the End

Most of the world's religions believe that death is not the end. They all agree that something normally called either consciousness or soul continues to exist in one form or another when it departs from the body. The body, on the other hand, is disposable. It dissolves back into the elements of which it was formed and becomes part and parcel of the earth which it inhabits.

Dr. R.N. Pernilla of Southampton General Hospital, U.K. found out that in patients experiencing cardiac arrest, when the brain stops functioning and they lose all reflexes, and when the EEG readings show that in ten seconds there is no brain activity on the surface or in the interior of the brain, 10 percent have reported near-death experiences. Therefore, he concludes that even after the brain stops functioning, there are signs of experiences, emotions, and memories that may be attributed to a mind or consciousness that exists independent of our brain, and that our brain is needed in order to manifest it.

The Facts of Life

As long as we are alive, the co-existence of our mind and soul in our body gives us the identity that we have. This same identity carries on throughout our lives, although both our bodies and our personalities undergo huge changes. We do not look the way we looked twenty, thirty, or forty years ago, nor do we feel or behave the same way, as we are subject to changes relative to all the other continuous changes around us.

The sense of solidity that we have throughout our lives about our bodies does not really exist outside the world of our thoughts. It is an idea or a self-image created by us and our social environment.

This self-image is only real to ourselves and nobody else, as it is only the product of our own thoughts and conviction.

At the moment of death, when the physical body separates from the soul, when the thought-producing brain ceases to function, all our bodily convictions and sense-related experiences and realities will cease to exist. The only experience that we will have will be that of our consciousness, of our spiritual awareness and the mental tendencies and experiences that we have created during our lives.

Heavens or Hell

If our mind or soul is peaceful, positive, and virtuous during our lives, then all our actions will follow suit with our minds. Hence, our actions and experiences will also be peaceful, positive, kind, and virtuous. We will have created a mind trained in the proper way through life. If our consciousness has been elevated to a consciousness of awareness of the Eternal Light, then at the time of death, when the mind is freed from the body and the influences of people and society have ceased to play a role, we will experience the states of peace and harmony of paradise in the next realm of eternal existence,

On the contrary, if during our earthly life we have trained and developed a mind or soul that is immersed in negative emotions, in hatred, jealousy, and anger, then this same mind that we will carry forward to eternity will still have the same burning feelings of rage, hatred, and anger.

Hell and paradise do not really exist as actual places, but as states of consciousness that our soul or mind experiences. We are experiencing these states partially while in this life and totally after death.

When a soul has an unclean conscience, it gets a taste of hell already on this Earth. On the contrary, feelings of peaceful mind, loving attitude, and joyful feelings create a state of paradise both in this life and the next.

Nothing in This Life Happens by Chance

Life is not a something that happens by chance. It is governed by certain laws and principles. A natural law of causation applies in our universe. Every action has a reaction, physicists teach us.

Every cause, mental or physical, initiates an effect. The Eastern cultures call it karma, the Greeks call it *pepromeno.* The word *pepromeno* comes from the verb *"pratto,"* which means "I do," so *pepromeno* means "what you have done"; in other words, your deeds and actions become your destiny.

Our destiny, our *pepromeno,* our karma are all reflections and reactions of our own thoughts, words, and deeds.

The very moment that we realize how our inner world directs our lives and afterlife, a greater way of living becomes available to us.

Every End Is Always Followed by a New Beginning

"........it is in dying that we are born to eternal life" St. Francis of Assisi.

During our earthly existence, every end is followed up by a new beginning. The cycle of pregnancy is followed by the beginning of life, and the end of life is followed by the beginning of the afterlife, which starts at the point of death.

During our lifetime, *"Ta panta rei,"* the ancient Greek philosophers used to say, translated literally it means "everything flows" or as a free translation it translates into "everything is changing continually".

All living things are subject to change and decay. Every moment is like a passage of changing events that start and end, followed by other events as we move between our birth to our death. We move through sunrises and sunsets, through happiness and sufferings, through successes and failures. Eventually, all good things not only come to an end but most often they become sources of pain and suffering too. This constitutes our life on Earth.

Socrates Considered Death to Be a Blessing

Socrates' thoughts about death were the following : Death can only be one of two things—either the dead are nothing and have no perception of anything or death is a relocation of the soul.

If death is a complete lack of perception, then death is like a dreamless sleep. Who can argue that a night of dreamless sleep is much better than most days and nights in one's life? Therefore, if death is a complete lack of perception, it is a blessing.

If death is a relocation of the soul, then Socrates thought that he would be spending his time talking with and examining the great figures of history and all others who have died already and have been relocated. That would give him extraordinary happiness. Therefore, if death is a relocation of the soul, it is still a blessing.

Rewards and Punishments

According to most cultures, we are trained by our parents, teachers, and society in general, to see the world and our existence in terms of right and wrong, good or evil, rewards and punishments. We are continually in fear of being blamed and accused by our fellow human beings, of being watched by the "all-seeing eye" and being judged by God.

Obviously, when we hold such a belief and we feel that we have not been virtuous but have sinned, at the time of death, we will be expecting to receive the most harsh judgment and punishment from God. In reality, it is not God that is punishing us but our conscience that will be following us after death as a state of consciousness.

Fortunately or unfortunately, all the things that we think, feel, and do leave an imprint in our consciousness, according to their nature. If they have been pure, we will have a positive imprint; if they have been wicked, we will have the most negative imprint.

How Can We Prepare for What's After Death?

King Solomon, after observing the cycles of life, noted that we human beings—knowing that death is inevitable—yearn for an eternal existence (Eccl. 12: 7-8)) and for a deeper meaning of life. The realization of death, of our mortality and the impermanence of this life, are normally the events that motivate us to think and prepare for our after-death existence.

All we know as human beings is that sooner or later, we will be dying, but we do not know when that will happen. We take it for granted that it will happen a very long time from now. If we forget about death, we will tend to forget the teachings, we will not be training our mind and have spiritual practices in order to elevate the consciousness of our awareness.

It is very important to know that while we are alive, we have the opportunity to create a healthy mind and consequently happy and blissful after-death conditions for ourselves by intense spiritual training, by continuous prayer and meditation.

At the time of death, it is very important to be praying to God, to be thinking of God's will and power solely, and to be meditating in God's name and presence exclusively, so that our minds are ready and in a condition to unite immediately with its infinite source.

Application

1- Believe in God and consider your after-death existence.

3- Give priority in your earthly life to all your spiritual goals and to your preparations for your afterlife.

2- Improve your intentions, dispel your negativities, give more emphasis in being good in mind, speech, and body and doing good in thought, word, or act.

4- Deflate your ego in order to become more tolerant and loving toward others.

Chapter 16

The Soul

And the dust returns to the earth as it was, and
the breath returns to God who gave it.

(ECCLESIASTES 12:7)

I strongly believe that one of the foundations of our faith is the belief in the immortality of the soul and in life after death. If one believes in God's existence, in God's justice, in miracles, in morality, and in other dimensions beyond our senses, one must also believe in the existence and in the immortality of the soul.

What Is the Soul?

All esotericism is based on the acceptance that there is a level of higher consciousness that lies beyond our mind, our intellect, and our ego; that it transcends space, time, cause, and effect; that it lies beyond what our senses can perceive, which we call soul or consciousness or essence.

In Genesis 2:7 we read, "And the LORD God formed man [of] the dust of the ground, and breathed into his nostrils the breath of life; and man became a living soul."

Socrates and Plato

Plato, drawing on the words of his teacher Socrates, considered the soul as the essence of a person. He considered this essence as an incorporeal, eternal occupant of our being, responsible for our behavior.

As bodies die, the soul is continually reborn in subsequent bodies. The Platonic soul comprises three parts: the mind, the emotion, and the desire. Each of these has a function in a balanced and peaceful soul.

Aristotle

Aristotle, following Plato, defined the soul as the core essence of a being, but argued against its having a separate existence. Unlike Plato and the religious traditions, Aristotle did not consider the soul as some kind of separate ghostly occupant of the body. As the soul, in Aristotle's view, is an actuality of a living body, it cannot be immortal.

Aristotle, however, makes it clear toward the end of his *De Anima* that he does believe that the intellect—which he considers to be a part of the soul—is eternal and separable from the body.

Christians regard the soul as the immortal essence of a human being, and they refer to the soul in a more moral rather than a philosophical way. They believe that when a person dies, his soul, which has been transformed by the good or evil deeds that the person has committed in his lifetime, will be judged by God as being worthy of eternal salvation or if he will suffer eternal separation from Him, the source of all good.

Higher Consciousness

The concept of higher consciousness claims that the average, ordinary human being goes through life only partially conscious of his eternal soul, due to the influences of external impulses and the preoccupations of daily life.

The physical body locks us into a frequency range, a lens through which we perceive the reality of the physical world only. As a result, most humans are considered to be asleep and living in the confusion of this life, seeing this reality as their only truth as they go about their daily business, instead of searching for their infinite consciousness or for their souls.

The Ultimate

God-consciousness and the activation of this energy which we call "the soul" is the need and goal of our existence in this world, and it should be the most longed-for and sought-after experience of a spiritual person.

In Christianity, this experience can occur as a result of prayer or as a religious experience given to the devotees by the grace of God, only.

Alternative Views

Avicenna, in his famous *Floating Man,* concludes that the idea of the real self is not logically dependent on any physical thing and that the soul should not be seen in relative terms.

This argument was later refined and simplified by René Descartes, who in epistemic terms stated: "I can abstract from the supposition of all external things but not from the supposition of my own consciousness."

The Soul Is Eternal

If the soul is a part of this undifferentiated energy from which all matter emerges mysteriously when life starts, and it breaks down into it again, when death occurs, then there is nothing to fear of death, as death is not "the nothingness" but "the everything-ness," and hell or paradise only exist as spiritual states that our soul experiences, and not as actual places.

If all matter is merely energy condensed to a slower vibration, then we are all one consciousness experiencing itself subjectively. Then there is no such thing as death. Life is just a dream, our reality is a frequency field experienced through the lens of a body, and we are all nothing but the imagination of ourselves.

Application

1- Realize that your soul is related to the vastness of this universe and that you are not a separate entity but a part of everything and fully connected with everything.

2- Experience the infinity of your soul and its potential to feel God, who lives inside our cells and throughout this universe.

3- Experience the life, the purity, the kindness, the love, the compassion, and the energy that resides inside your soul in order to experience God in you.

4- Through your prayers, through your meditative state, and through your devotional acts, try to match the frequency of the vibrations of your soul with the frequencies vibrated throughout the universe, in order to experience God, who permeates this universe.

Chapter 17

_____

Christian Morality

Then he called the crowd again and said to them, 'Listen to me, all
of you, and understand: there is nothing outside a person that by
going in can defile, but the things that come out are what defile.'
When he had left the crowd and entered the house, his disciples
asked him about the parable. He said to them, 'Then do you also fail
to understand? Do you not see that whatever goes into a person
from outside cannot defile, since it enters, not the heart but the
stomach, and goes out into the sewer?' And he said, 'It is what comes
out of a person that defiles. For it is from within, from the human
heart, that evil intentions come: fornication, theft, murder, adultery,
avarice, wickedness, deceit, licentiousness, envy, slander, pride, folly.
All these evil things come from within, and they defile a person.

(MARK 7:14-23)

Based on my studies in sociology and anthropology, I noticed
that "morality" is a peculiar word. People normally talk about
morality as a relative term, rather than as an absolute term. We
have, for example, the Christian morality, the Jewish morality, the
morality of the different cultures and geographic regions, or the
morality of the ancient Greeks. In other words, morality seems to
be a code of conduct that we as members of a certain society or
ethnic group or religion put forward for a certain period of time.
Eventually, this sense of morality will change with time or as a result
of some big events like wars or catastrophes.

What Is Morality?

Morality is a system of standards and behavior. It evokes in us a sense of moral responsibility from which the voice of our conscience originates and our moral profile gets formed.

Morality and Decision-making

Our sense of morality plays a very important role in our everyday decisions. It shapes our behavior as we go through our days and conduct our business.

We often have to compromise our morality at a personal level, in order either to avoid trouble or for personal justifications and for personal gains, or at a social level for a collective apparent well-being.

On What Is Morality Based?

Morality is most often relative to a culture, and it is based on the legal and the religious belief system of the people. In most systems, normally, morality is based on virtue and on what is considered to be virtuous. In Judaism, for example, virtue and virtuous living means obedience to the Mosaic Law and living according to the commandments. There is no halfway measure; one is either obedient or not, virtuous or not, either good or bad, evil or holy. The good and virtuous eventually get compensated by salvation, and the non-virtuous get punished by suffering.

What Do Christians Do?

Christians too, in a very simplistic and most Judaic way, most often feel that if they have not committed one of the major transgressions prescribed in the Ten Commandments, and they have fasted, that they are worthy of receiving Holy Communion as a reward for their virtuous behavior. Yet, we read in the Divine Liturgy that no one is worthy of the Holy Communion in spite of any virtuous living or fasting and praying preparation. Only by the grace of God we become able to participate in the Body of Christ, the Word, and have a chance of transforming our human nature into the likeness of God.

What Is Christianity?

Christianity is a religion based on truth, the true Word, and true living. The Christian life is based on principles, which are standards of conduct. The Christian principles of truth, forgiveness, compassion, and love lead one in the direction of higher consciousness of understanding, of receiving, and of giving the goodness of life.

When you transform your consciousness by expanding your awareness, your perception of everyday life changes and you experience the presence of the divine in your life. This is the gift of the divine grace, which lights our path by working through our intuition and by guiding the choices we make.

If we want to be true representatives of our Christian faith, then the oneness of this Creation and the oneness of God should be reflected by us. Every part of us should be united. There should be no separation between body, mind, soul, and spirit.

It is this integration of all those four elements that gives us the good health, the energy, and the strength to stand and sail through this world in peace through our devotion, commitment, and faith.

What Does Christianity Teach?

Christian doctrine is not based upon the dualistic system of right and wrongdoing, or on virtues, but rather on being truthful with oneself, inside one's heart and mind. It is not what one does that is important but who one is, not just conforming to the law but believing in it.

Doing something is an external, pride-producing, and ego-inflating practice, leading consequently to feelings of superiority and self-righteousness, which is the exact opposite of what any Christian should try to achieve. Jesus, in the parable of the Pharisee and the tax collector (Luke 10–14), spoke about some people who are so confident of their own righteousness and so very proud of themselves for keeping the Mosaic Law and helping the poor that they look down upon everyone else.

Christian morality is based only in truth. Jesus said "I am the way, and the truth, and the life. No one comes to the Father except through me." (John 14:6).

Christian morality has to do with the person's real self, his actual identity, and not the roles he plays in society and the masks he wears in order to be accepted and praised by his fellow human beings.

What Are Truth, Love, and Goodness?

Truth, love, and goodness, as attributes of the soul, are the only important components in a Christian's life.

Truth is our Lord Jesus, His life, teachings, and example. He is the ultimate revelation of the nature of God on Earth.

Love is the creative energy of this universe. God is love, both in essence and energy. The matching relationship between this divine love and human love is what results in morality and what any Christian should strive for.

Goodness is produced when human elevated awareness and human reality matches the divine truth, the divine will, and the divine good.

Good in Christianity is identified with God. "Why do you ask me about what is good? None is good except God," Jesus said (Matthew 19:16). Accordingly, anything that matches to the divine good is good for oneself and others, it is moral and it is ethical.

What Is the Christian Morality?

Christian morality is living and acting as close as possible according to standards laid down by Jesus. It is not "what God wants us to do," which relates to obedience but rather "what would Jesus do" that should determine our actions as an act of faithful imitation.

Jesus said to His disciples:

Then he called the crowd again and said to them, 'Listen to me, all of you, and understand: there is nothing outside a person that by going in can defile, but the things that come out are what defile.'

When he had left the crowd and entered the house, his disciples asked him about the parable. He said to them, 'Then do you also fail to understand? Do you not see that whatever goes into a person from outside cannot defile, since it enters, not the heart but the stomach, and goes out into the sewer?' (Thus he declared all foods clean.) And he said, 'It is what comes out of a person that defiles. For it is from within, from the human heart, that evil intentions come: fornication, theft, murder, adultery, avarice, wickedness, deceit, licentiousness, envy, slander, pride, folly. All these evil things come from within, and they defile a person.' (Mark7:14-23)

What Is the Purpose of Morality?

The purpose of the Christian morality is not to improve one's outward behavior. It is an inner action of transforming one's mind and reason in order to achieve a higher consciousness of awareness of the divine truth and to live according to it. In this way, one can establish a communion between oneself and God to the point of the ultimate union called **theosis.**

Application

1- Do not do unto others what you do not want others to do unto you.

2- Carry each other's burdens.

3- Love your neighbor like yourself.

Chapter 18

Religion

And I tell you, you are Peter, and on this rock I will build my church, and the gates of Hades will not prevail against it.

(MATTHEW 16:18)

Religion, in my humble opinion, is the world's largest, the most functional, and the most organized social structure, which deals with the human need for spirituality and its yearning for immortality.

Through ritualistic practices, through prayers, through symbolism, and through supernatural narratives referring to a Higher Power, all religions in this world have helped humanity tremendously and beyond any doubt, in its search to find meaning in this life, to enjoy greater personal security, to achieve better health and in general, to lead happier lives with better human relationships.

We all know that when religions get manipulated by politics, they become a deadly threat to humanity, defeating their actual spiritual function of promoting spirituality and spreading love, goodness, and peace.

Christianity is one of the world's biggest religions, with about 2.5 billion followers worldwide. It is based on the teachings of Jesus Christ, who lived in the Holy Land two thousand years ago.

The Church

When Jesus asked Peter, 'Who do people say that the Son of Man is?' And they said, 'Some say John the Baptist, but others

Elijah, and still others Jeremiah or one of the prophets.' He said to them, 'But who do you say that I am?' Simon Peter answered, 'You are the Messiah, the Son of the living God.' And Jesus answered him, 'Blessed are you, Simon son of Jonah! For flesh and blood has not revealed this to you, but my Father in heaven. And I tell you, you are Peter, and on this rock I will build my church, and the gates of Hades will not prevail against it." (Matthew16:13-19) That is the first time the word "Church" was mentioned over 2,000 years ago.

What Did Jesus Do?

Human societies are structured according to certain systems of thought and action that we call *principles*. Our principles influence our daily behavior, and they constitute our culture. Jesus, with His teachings and His new way of thinking, challenged all those very human structures that existed in his time. He proclaimed a new relationship with God. He knew that the new way of life that He was promoting and His teachings were drastically different than what the others in His time were teaching. He knew that the religious institutions of His time were not conducive to God's revelation. His parable of the wine skins was destined to be a warning against this.

Wine in those days was normally placed in animal skins in order to ferment. New wines were placed in new skins because new skins have the ability to expand in order to accommodate the gases and the pressure created during the fermentation process, while old wine was placed in the old skins, which are dry and brittle, with no elasticity and no capacity to expand.

Jesus taught new ideas and new principles of truth to people who had an old way of life and an old religion. He taught that some old ideas were like the old skins, too rigid and too dry to contain His new teachings of a new kingdom and a new order. People had become too much set in their ways and their laws. They had closed their minds to new ideas about God and how He reveals Himself to His people. Cultural rituals prevailed devotion.

What Is Happening Today

Has our own faith perhaps become dry and brittle too? Have our cultural rituals prevailed over our devotion? Do we perhaps continue our old ways of practicing without thinking, as change requires effort and it is not as comfortable, easy, and predictable?

Have our own spiritual lives lost their elasticity to accommodate the Spirit of God? Do we stick to the old structures and principles automatically without considering a new way of thinking and acting based on the writings of the fathers of our Church, in order to receive spiritual enlightenment?

Have we become so absorbed by the details in our religion that we have lost the most valuable truths on which it is all based?

Have we perhaps confused the truth of God's Word, which is constantly being revealed to us, with the traditions and regulations of the structure that holds it? The truth is not in the wine skin but in the new wine, which symbolizes Jesus' teachings to us.

The Church as an Organization

Unfortunately, when the Church became an organization rather than a movement for spiritual development and higher consciousness, some of Jesus' teachings lost their meaning, as for many Christians, the traditions, laws, and regulations of the structure of the Church became primary and the teachings of the gospel secondary.

Unfortunately, all the Christian churches are subject to the parable of the wine. Unfortunately the wine skins, in our days too, have become more important than the wine. Some Christian churches still spread the truth of Jesus' teaching in a way and a language that no one can understand, and no one is getting any benefit or excitement from it.

The joy of the good news of the gospel gets wasted in an archaic form of worship that has no relevance to young people.

The continuous illumination of the Holy Spirit is continuously expanding with God's love like the new wine, and we must expand with it.

Conclusion

The duty and obligation of the Church should be to promote the gospel, the love, the humility, and the compassion that is required of Christians, and to constantly change and renew itself in order to hold the truth of God's ever-expanding love for us.

Application

1- Never substitute the Word (Jesus Christ) for the organization (Church) that promotes the teachings.

2- Never forget that only the truth of the teachings of Jesus can radically change human lives irrespective of through which denomination one gets exposed to them.

3- Trust, love, and have faith in God and not in human structures and human hierarchies. These keep fighting and competing with each other, creating animosity between the very same church of our Jesus Christ.

Chapter 19

Conclusion

The main idea of this book is about God.

When we consciously become aware of the existence of God, we come to realize that God is the only reality of our being. This realization has a transforming effect in our lives. It helps us create a more harmonious self, a more harmonious family, and a more harmonious society in which peace and joy prevail.

If we consciously believe that we come to this life with a purpose and that our purpose is to serve humanity, to raise our consciousness, and to receive the grace of God, we become connected to the universal light, and through it, we can gain universal consciousness of awareness.

If we have faith and if we let the grace infiltrate our being, then our life, through our relationship with God, becomes a state of bliss and ecstasy.

AMEN

Thoughts to Ponder On

It is no mark of intelligence to be able to prove whatever one pleases. But to be able to discern what is true as true and what is false as false—this is the mark and character of intelligence.

—Emmanuel Swedenborg (1678–1772)

I was brought up to believe that the only thing worth doing was to add to the sum of accurate information in the world.

—Margaret Mead

What Is Wisdom?

Wisdom is the realization of insights at a deeper level. It is the ability to see things as they are by our logic and reasoning and not through our perception, which is based in our senses and interpreted by our mental faculties or through our illusions, which are based in our automatic thinking processes.

Wisdom is not the same as intelligence. It is possible to have great intelligence but very little wisdom. Higher moral disciplines by practicing virtuous acts and avoiding the non-virtuous ones, together with higher concentration levels, lead to higher wisdom.

What Is Perfection?

The greatest perfection we can ever reach is by becoming true to ourselves and other people. No mastery is greater than mastering ourselves and our own passions.

One needs good character, intelligence, and good judgment in order to perfect oneself.

Perfection is not in quantity but in quality. "Do not rely on the opinion of the many but of the one and the expert," Socrates used to tell the Athenians. If you are going to rely on the opinions of others totally, what is the use of having your own?

What Is Humility?

We should try daily to elevate our taste, fill our words with wisdom and our deeds with prudence. Then our superiority will always be evident.

Handling our superiority with humility and serenity will make us lovable to our inferiors and not competitive to our superiors.

When helping someone with advice, pretend to be reminding him of something he has forgotten and not telling him something he does not know.

Advice is sometimes accepted much more readily through a joke or an example rather than through teaching.

Secrets

Do not share your plans and your secrets with others. A more private life is a happier life, while fame requires continuous work and effort. You are as much as you know. Knowledge and honorable intentions offer you immortality and praise, as people always remember your knowledge and wisdom.

Never testify against your own good taste and principles in order to please others. Let your own integrity keep you righteous.

Friends

Associate with those you can learn from, either by example or by words. When your friends become your teachers, then you will be combining learning with pleasure.

When you are surrounded by a circle of people of great understanding and wisdom, you can use their knowledge and experience when needed. Unfortunately, we have a short life and much to learn. It is impossible for one person to know more than what many may know.

Often, mediocre people who apply themselves go much further than intelligent people who do not.

Application depends on temperament, hard work produces good results, and good fortune is helped along by much effort and virtue.

Plans

When you start something, do not share your plans with others and do not raise people's expectations. Whatever gets praised before it has started seldom materializes, because it can never measure up to its expectations.

No matter how excellent something is, it can never measure up to imagination and hence to expectations, so the final result ends up being more disappointing than admirable.

You can win more admiration by keeping people guessing the extent of your talent, intelligence, and knowledge than you can by displaying it.

Reason

Side with reason and do not occupy yourselves with small and insignificant things and people. *No activity* is better than useless and high-risk activity.

Bad luck is often brought on by stupidity, as most often, one evil deed is followed by many. Fools are lost by not thinking and by paying much attention to what matters the least and little attention to what matters the most.

Moderation

Exercise moderation in everything you do, especially in your dealings with others. In this way, you will keep their esteem, which is precious, for much longer.

Keep out of dangerous and extreme situations. Dangerous situations place our judgment in jeopardy, and one dangerous situation often leads to another. Often it is more courageous to avoid danger than to try to face it. Don't be proud of being envied.

Emotions

Never hurry, and never give way to your emotions. Master yourself in order to master others. Great worth requires great work; only perfection is noticed and only success endures, while mediocrity never wins applause.

Distinction is not the cause of affection and love; only good deeds are. Do not yield to every sort of passing thought. Do not hold on to anger and negativity. Develop sensitivity and compassion for the difficulties and pain of others.

Self-correction starts with self-knowledge. Know your character, intellect, judgment, and emotions. You cannot master yourself if you do not understand yourself. The mirror of the spirit is wise self-reflection.

Choices

Be very careful about your choices, as most things in life depend on the choices we make. Our choices depend on our judgment, intelligence, and diligence.

Recognize your special attributes and cultivate them in order to excel in them and achieve respect. Avoid both contradicting others or being contradicted.

Never do something out of stubbornness, but out of careful reflection. It is not prudent to act on probability. Good common sense is a gift from heaven.

Flattery

Often flattery offered by false friends is more dangerous than criticism spoken by enemies. Criticism corrects the faults which flattery disguises.

Class

Man is born a barbarian. Culture raises him above the beast, into a true and a great person.

There is nothing more cultivating than knowledge, followed by refinement and polish. Some people show a natural refinement both in their concepts and words, aspiring to elevation, acting courteously in a noble manner, while others are gross, tarnishing everything around them.

Truth

Be truthful in your communication with others, as your words affect your mind, which affects your body, your health, and your environment.

Bibliography

The Holy Bible New Revised Standard Version Bible, copyright 1989, Division of Christian Education of the National Council of the Churches of Christ in the United States of America

Philokalia: The Eastern Christian Spiritual Texts by G. E. H. Palmer, Philip Sherrard, and Kallistos (2006).

Confronting and Controlling Thoughts: According to the Fathers of the Philokalia by Anthony M. Coniaris (2004).

Reason for God by Timothy Keller (2008).

The Essential Writings of Christian Mysticism by Bernard Mcginn (paperback, 2006).

Entering the Castle by Caroline Myss. 2008

Seeing with the Eyes of Love: Reflections on a Classic of Christian Mysticism by Eknath Easwaran (1991).

The Origin and Nature of Matter and Consciousness by Jeff Love (1979).

Infinity and the Mind by Rudy Rucker (1979).

St. John of the Cross and Dr. C.G. Jung: Christian Mysticism in the Light of Jungian Psychology by Jim Arraj (1986).

Aristotle's Metaphysics (2000).

Son of Man by Andrew Harvey 1999

Christian Mysticism: The Art of the Inner Way by William McNamara (1991).

The Inner Journey —Views from the Christian Tradition, edited by Lorraine Kisley. 2006

The Dalai Lama's Book of Love and Compassion (2001).

The Power of Positive Thinking by Norman Vincent Peale (1953).

Great Dialogues of Plato (1984).

The Practice of the Presence of God by Brother Lawrence of the Resurrection 1982

Meditation, The Art of Ecstacy by Bhagwan S. Rajneesh (1980).

Elder Paisios of the Holy Mountain by Priestmionk Christodoulos Ageloglou (1993).

A Book of Saints by James Cochrane 2001

Oh God Why? by Gerard W. Hughes 2002

The Power of Now by Eckhart Tolle (2006).

A New Model of the Universe by P. D. Ouspensky (1932)

Spiritual Interpretation of Scripture by Joel Goldsmith (1999)

Practicing the Presence by Joel S. Goldsmith 1984

The Be Happy Attitudes by Dr. Robert Schuller (1996)

Cosmic Consciousness by Richard Maurice Bucke. 1992

The Quantum Gods—The Origin and Nature of Matter and Consciousness by Jeff Love 1976